Designing and Building Business Models Using Microsoft Excel

D1635780

Designing and Building Business Models Using Microsoft Excel

Andrew J. Robson
University of Northumbria at Newcastle

McGRAW-HILL BOOK COMPANY

London · New York · St Louis · San Francisco · Auckland · Bogotá · Caracas · Lisbon
Mexico · Milan · Montreal · New Delhi · Panama · Paris · San Juan · São Paulo · Singapore
Sydney · Tokyo · Toronto

Published by
McGRAW-HILL Book Company Europe
Shoppenhangers Road, Maidenhead, Berkshire SL6 2QL, England
Telephone 01628 23432
Fax 01628 770224

British Library Cataloguing in Publication Data
Robson, Andrew J.
  Designing and Building Business Models
  Using Microsoft Excel
  I. Title
  005.369

  ISBN 0-07-709058-6

Library of Congress Cataloging-in-Publication Data
Robson, Andrew J.
    Designing and building business models using Microsoft Excel /
  Andrew J. Robson.
        p.   cm.
    Includes index.
    ISBN 0-07-709058-6 (pbk. : alk. paper)
    1. Microsoft Excel (Computer file) 2. Business—Mathematical
  models—Computer programs. 3. Business—Decision making
  Mathematical models—Computer programs. I. Title.
  HF5548.4.M523R62 1995
  005.369—dc20   95-6597
                                                                         CIP

2 3 4 5 BB 2 1 0

Printed and bound in Great Britian by Bell & Bain Ltd. Glasgow

CONTENTS

For many students and business decision-makers there has been an increase in the use of personal computers and related software. This is especially true for students studying on Information Technology (IT), Computing and Business related courses. In particular, the spreadsheet has become both popular and widely accepted in business and higher education. In the business world, the popularity of the spreadsheet can be explained by its inherent 'user-friendliness' and because it affords the decision-maker with an environment in which a range of scenarios can be considered quickly and easily. By exploiting this 'user-friendly' environment, many decision-makers have gained a greater insight into various problems encountered within their business.

A number of decision-makers have also recognized the advantages of developing business models using the spreadsheet, many being formal and structured in nature. However, many of these models are badly designed, often because their development has taken place in a piecemeal manner. As a consequence, the resultant models are often difficult to use and understand. The problems encountered during model development arise primarily because the modeller is inadequately trained in either modelling techniques or spreadsheet operations.

In contrast, the need to structure high-level programs is both widely accepted and practised, and a number of textbooks describe structured programming using languages such as Fortran and Pascal. The objective of this book is to define an equivalent structured approach for the development of formal spreadsheet models. In describing a structured approach to spreadsheet modelling, it is hoped that the reader will go on to develop models which are usable, efficient and easy to amend. The ideas described in this book are readily applicable to those modellers who wish to build formal business models for end users who may have little spreadsheet experience. However, by describing a formal approach to modelling, it is *not* intended to deter those who simply wish to exploit the informality offered by the spreadsheet when undertaking tasks such as creating graphs and performing simple 'one-off' calculations.

This book is aimed at those students undertaking courses in spreadsheet modelling, and these are likely to be either from a Business or a Computing background. The concepts can be adopted by students at both undergraduate and postgraduate level. In this book, reference will be made to one spreadsheet, namely Microsoft Excel (version 4). However, the book does not include detailed command sequences, which have been omitted in order to keep the text as general as possible. In doing so, the concepts described are readily applicable and transferable to other spreadsheets offering the appropriate facilities; in particular those spreadsheets which are mouse/icon rather than command driven. In describing a structured approach to modelling, the book does not provide a detailed description of major modelling techniques, but refers to a simple business problem so that the reader can focus clearly on the major concepts of model design. By referring to a simple model throughout the book, it is hoped to develop a set of 'good practice' guidelines which can be used whenever a formal spreadsheet model needs to be developed. For the reader who is interested in specific modelling techniques, there are a number of additional texts which may be referenced. In writing this book, the author has assumed that the reader has both a basic knowledge of spreadsheet operations and certain well-established quantitative techniques.

The concepts of formal model development are introduced in this book in a sequential manner, chapter by chapter. At the end of each chapter are 'review questions' which aim to test the reader's understanding of the concepts introduced and 'case study questions' which allow the reader to put the ideas considered into practice. The 'case study questions' pertain to a specific modelling application and, when completed, the reader should have developed a structured, user-friendly spreadsheet model, incorporating all of the 'good practices' set out in this book.

INTRODUCTION TO SPREADSHEET MODELLING

OVERVIEW

This chapter shows how a business model can be developed using the power and capabilities of a modern spreadsheet and, in doing so, introduces the concept of (formal) spreadsheet modelling. Additionally, it highlights how the inherent properties of the spreadsheet may unfortunately result in the development of a badly structured model. A systematic approach to building formal models, which forms the basis of this book, is then described.

OBJECTIVES

After reading this chapter and working through the questions, the reader will be able to:

- Define and understand the term 'model'.
- Distinguish between the different types of model that can be developed.
- Identify the intrinsic features of the spreadsheet.
- Recognize how the spreadsheet provides an informal environment in which models can be developed, but how this informality may result in a badly structured model.
- Recognize the essential features of a formal business model.
- Recognize a systematic approach to building a formal spreadsheet model, but be aware that relationships between the different stages in the modelling process may be iterative rather than sequential.

INTRODUCTION

For many decision-makers there has been an increase in both the use of personal computers (PCs) and associated software. One particular area of growth has been in the business sector. Managers and workers in this area use PCs regularly and the spreadsheet has proved itself to be highly popular.

Whereas some personnel have used spreadsheets to create graphs and perform 'one-off' calculations, a number of others also understand the benefit of developing formal business models. Quite often, many of the models developed are badly structured and, as a consequence, can be difficult to use, maintain or amend. Problematic models often arise because they are developed in a piecemeal manner (this will be illustrated later in this chapter) and also because many spreadsheet modellers have little or no formal computer training. Moreover, a number of these modellers may fail to appreciate the need to plan both the structure and contents of a formal model.

This chapter introduces the concept of formal spreadsheet modelling and describes how a spreadsheet model can be developed. The informality of the spreadsheet is considered and the chapter demonstrates how this 'user-friendliness' may unfortunately result in a badly structured model. Once a badly structured model has been considered, a systematic approach to the formal modelling process is addressed towards the end of the chapter. In doing so, a number of interrelated stages in this process are identified, and these steps form the basis of the book.

Throughout this book two categories of personnel will be referred to. The first category is the 'modeller' who is responsible for developing, testing and validating any formal model, and the second is the 'end user' or 'model user' who will use the model as a tool in the decision-making process.

DEFINITION OF A MODEL

Before considering the features of the spreadsheet and, in turn, the spreadsheet modelling process, it is important for the reader to understand what is meant by the term 'model'. Quite simply, a model is a simplified illustration of a real situation. Moreover, a model can be either a descriptive or prescriptive representation. Descriptive models are used to describe either an existing or desired situation, and, in doing so, these models (if successful) provide the end user with an opportunity to explore a number of different scenarios. Additionally, a descriptive model allows an end user to ask 'what if' questions about the situation under consideration. An example of a descriptive modelling technique is simulation. In contrast, prescriptive models are deterministic in nature and these models often include the use of algorithms. The aim of a prescriptive model is to provide the model user with a 'best' answer to the problem under consideration. An example of a prescriptive modelling technique is linear programming (LP) which uses the simplex algorithm. The LP model contains an objective (i.e. what the end user wishes to achieve) and if it is used, say, to model a production problem, then the 'best' solution indicates a product mix which either maximizes profits or minimizes costs.

In general, there are a number of advantages in modelling a problem as well as a number of shortcomings. In particular, the advantage of building a model is that a greater understanding of a business problem can be afforded, and, coupled with the expertise and experience of the model user, this can facilitate effective decision-making. In contrast, the model user should be made aware that the model is only a simplification of reality, and, as a consequence, the resultant output generated by a model represents perhaps only one of a number of possibilities.

The model should *never* replace the experience and expertise of the end user, but supplement it. That is, the model should assist the end user, but not act as a substitute.

CATEGORIES OF MODEL

Although a model can provide either a descriptive or prescriptive insight into a business problem, it generally belongs to one of four main categories:

- An *analog* model involves representing the properties of the problem under consideration by distinct features of the model. An example of an analog model is an ordnance survey map which uses contours as a measurement of height.
- A *conceptual* model is used primarily to transform the problem under consideration into a mathematical model. In reality, a conceptual model is a diagrammatical display of the

problem. Conceptual modelling utilizes techniques such as influence diagrams which are described in detail in Chapter 2.

- An *iconic* model is a physical and (usually) scaled representation of a problem. A simple example of an iconic model is a model railway which may be used to represent an actual rail network. Iconic models were particularly useful before computers became widely available when the modelling capabilities of the computer were less sophisticated.

- A *mathematical* model uses mathematical formulae to describe the relationships that exist between the different variables in the problem under consideration. These variables and their associated interrelationships can be identified during the development of a conceptual model. Moreover, the spreadsheet provides an environment in which the formulae identified can be constructed. 'Business-related' models which fall into this category include statistical models such as time series forecasting techniques and financial models such as the net present value (NPV) technique which can be used to determine the viability of a future investment.

APPLICATION OF SPREADSHEETS TO MODELLING

For many decision-makers, the use of PCs and associated software has steadily increased. Together with the increase in access to relevant numerical data, this has resulted in an increase in model building. Additionally, the *spreadsheet* has become an accepted piece of application software.

A large number of business personnel like the spreadsheet mainly because of its intrinsic user-friendliness and also because it provides an 'informal' environment in which they can use and develop models. Specifically, it is easy to enter data onto a spreadsheet and quickly construct graphs and perform 'one-off' calculations. For a modeller possessing greater skill and experience, the spreadsheet can be used to develop larger business models, many of which may have to be structured and formal in nature.

THE SPREADSHEET

Whatever spreadsheet is employed, the modeller should be aware of a common structure and appearance. In simplistic terms, a spreadsheet is a software program which consists of rows and columns of cells which combine to form a grid or worksheet. The spreadsheet is user-friendly in appearance and is readily accessible, even to those model users with limited computing experience. From the point of view of the modeller, one advantage of developing a model using a spreadsheet is that the formulae which form the basis of many business models can be executed both quickly and automatically. Specifically, each cell on the spreadsheet grid can contain text, numbers or formulae which can be combined appropriately by the modeller to develop a formal business model. Because the spreadsheet is informal, the resultant model can be used by end users with varying computing experience. This book assumes that the reader is capable of using basic spreadsheet operations such as entering text, numbers and formulae, creating graphs and undertaking business calculations; as a consequence, these subjects will only be considered briefly here.

Additionally, it is assumed that the reader is aware that many spreadsheets provide built-in functions which can be readily incorporated into a formal business model. Perhaps the simplest example of such a function is **AVERAGE( )** (offered by Microsoft Excel) which can be used to calculate the mean value of a data set.

In this book, reference is made to one spreadsheet, namely Microsoft Excel. However, with the exception of the description of macro code, detailed command sequences have not been included. These have been omitted in order to keep the text as general as possible. Thus the concepts described are readily applicable and transferable to other spreadsheets offering the appropriate facilities; in particular those spreadsheets which are mouse/icon rather than command driven.

Whereas all spreadsheet modellers will be able to write text, numbers and formulae onto a spreadsheet and combine these to develop a 'model', it may not be apparent that the model is badly structured and, as a consequence, not user-friendly. Many modellers will simply start building the model in the top left-hand corner of the spreadsheet (cell A1), perhaps paying little attention to the layout and appearance of the resultant code. A model developed in this way will be difficult to amend if changes occur to the situation being modelled. Moreover, by programming in this way, little regard has been made to the needs of the end user, who may have little experience of spreadsheets. This can be illustrated by a simple example.

The manager of a commercial decorating company wishes to predict the duration and costs of future contracts. The manager has no previous experience of using a spreadsheet, but nevertheless would like a simple model to be developed. The input requirements for this simple model are the length, width and height of a building in addition to the number of doors and windows. Using this information, the area of the building can be calculated, from which the contract's duration and cost can be determined. The spreadsheet model developed is illustrated in Figure 1.1.

The simple model contains all of the necessary calculations, which have been unambiguously labelled on-screen. However, the model illustrated is actually badly structured. The screen shown in Figure 1.1 consists of input data (building dimensions and appropriate hourly rate), processes (calculations) and output (contract time and cost). The main problem with the model presented above is that these different functional areas overlap on-screen, as depicted in Figure 1.2.

	A	B	C	D	E	F	G	H	I
1									
2									
3									
4		Length of the building:			12		Area:	345	
5									
6		Width of the building:			10		Time:	15.49	
7									
8		Height of the building:			9				
9									
10		Number of Doors:			1				
11									
12		Number of Windows:			2				
13									
14									
15		Hourly Rate:			11.50				
16									
17		Cost:			178.14				
18									

Figure 1.1 Construction of a (simple) spreadsheet model

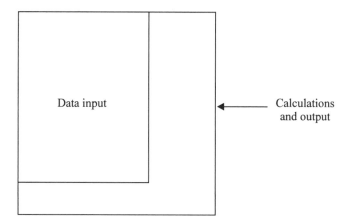

Figure 1.2 Overlapping areas in the badly constructed model

An overlap of data input and calculations can prove particularly problematic for an end user with limited spreadsheet experience. One of the greatest sources of user error is caused by over-writing a model's code (in particular its formulae) during data input. If a model has a structure like that represented by Figure 1.2, there is an increased chance of this occurring.

In general, the spreadsheet will permit changes to the model (perhaps addition or deletion of certain input variables or formulae), and in the absence of a predetermined structure the structural changes are likely to be performed in a piecemeal manner. In the simple example illustrated, the mix of input, process and output is unlikely to prove problematic, especially if the end user is provided with a comprehensive set of instructions. However, in the development of a larger, non-trivial model, a predetermined structure will be vital, particularly if the model's structure and contents need to be responsive to changes in the problem under consideration. Specifically, a model structured like that illustrated in Figure 1.2 will prove difficult to amend because the main functional areas overlap. In general, where an application is large and non-trivial, an increase in code will result in an increase in potential problems for both modeller and end user.

The best approach to spreadsheet modelling is to harness the informality and user-friendliness that the software provides (i.e. the ease with which graphs and formulae can be constructed and results generated both quickly and accurately), but at the same time adopt a structure which is adaptable to change and is agreeable to model users with varying spreadsheet expertise. The most apparent improvement that could be made to the simple model shown in Figure 1.1 would be to ensure that the main functional areas of data input, process and output remain separate and self-contained. This would make the model adaptable to expansion (if ever necessary) and ensure that the end user does not inadvertently corrupt the model code.

A second improvement could be made to the model illustrated in Figure 1.1 which is equally important but perhaps less apparent. While the model incorporates unambiguous labelling, there is no on-screen help provision which can be accessed by the model user. Again, for more complex models, on-screen support for the end user will become increasingly important.

In short, the model user should be provided with a formal structure which consists of:

• The functional areas of the model which are presented on-screen as separate, self-contained sections

- On-screen support facilities

The subsequent chapters of this book will describe the role of both areas in a formal model structure by reference to a simple, but formal, spreadsheet model. Moreover, by developing a formal model, the author will describe how the end user's requirements have been met.

THE (SPREADSHEET) MODELLING PROCESS

In developing a formal model, one of a number of accepted approaches may be taken. The approach taken in this book is sequential in nature, where the modelling process is assumed to consist of a number of interrelated stages. At each stage in the modelling process, a set of 'good practice' guidelines is provided. That is, a simple modelling scenario will be considered, with emphasis on the content, layout and presentation of the required features. To provide a structure for the book, it has been assumed that one stage leads directly to another. In the development of a number of more complex business models, assuming a sequential approach may be unrealistic. Instead, the modelling process may prove to be highly iterative.

For simplicity, the stages to be considered in this book are:

- Problem conceptualization and data analysis (*Chapter 2*)
- Model design (*Chapter 3*)
- Spreadsheet development of the model (*Chapter 4*)
- Model automation (*Chapter 5*)
- Validation and verification of the model (*Chapter 6*)
- Model documentation (*Chapter 7*)
- Implementation and use of the model (*Chapter 8*)

Figure 1.3 illustrates how these stages are related. However, the reader must remember that as a modelling application becomes more complex, the steps are less likely to be sequential. For example, in testing the validity of the model, the modeller may decide that it cannot operate to a desired level of accuracy. In response to this problem, more data may have to be collected and further analysis undertaken. In short, this shows how the process is iterative rather than sequential between the stages of problem conceptualization and model validation. That is, the data is collected and the modelling process is undertaken until the validation stage (as shown in Figure 1.3). At this point the modeller may consider that additional data is required. This data would be subsequently collected and analysed, and model construction and testing would be undertaken once again. The model would then be re-validated, the results determining whether the model has become sufficiently representative of the problem under consideration.

ESSENTIAL FEATURES OF A MODEL

In general, any model developed using the approach illustrated in Figure 1.3 is a simplification of reality and, as a result, is usually less complex than the actual (business) situation. Nevertheless, the model should be comprehensive in the relationships it considers and subsequently represents. If these ideals are achieved, the model can be considered to be representative of the (business) situation. In addition to a model being representative, the modeller needs to ensure that the resultant program is:

- *Easy to use and maintain, and, whenever appropriate, easy to amend.* Moreover, a model should be responsive to changes in the real-life business process. These changes may be easier to make (i.e. the model is easy to use) if the model's parameters are located 'outside' its

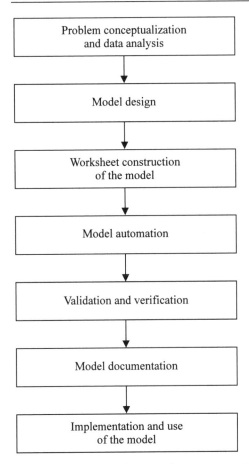

Figure 1.3   Sequential approach to structured spreadsheet modelling

internal processes and calculations. That is, the functional areas of data input, process and output remain separate and self-contained. A user-friendly structure may be achieved in a spreadsheet model by using a framework based on self-contained blocks of cells. By using such a structure, this will ensure that the contents of an individual block can be amended easily in response to any change in the business problem without major disruption to the rest of the model. In contrast, the simple model illustrated in Figure 1.1 may prove difficult to amend because the functional sections overlap. For example, if the company introduced a discount scheme where the hourly rate charged depended upon the contract duration, a number of hourly rates may have to be coded into the model. Given the location of the hourly rate in the present model, this may result in a (relatively) significant structural change. An appropriate model structure will be introduced and described fully in Chapter 3.

- *Comprehensively documented* and understandable both to the modeller and end user. The documentation of a model is a requirement not only for the end user but also for those modelling personnel charged with maintaining and amending the model. The model shown in Figure 1.1 is badly documented since the end user is provided with no on-screen help facility and there is no spreadsheet description of the formulae used. Model documentation is described fully in Chapter 7.

• *Cost-effective*. That is, the cost of constructing, validating, testing and using the model should generally not exceed any monetary savings made by the organization. However, in many modelling situations, the benefits of developing a business model may be non-tangible, and so the success of its development and implementation may rely heavily upon the negotiating skills of the modelling personnel.

CONCLUSIONS

At the beginning of this chapter, the categories of model which may be developed and the implicit features they incorporate were defined. Specifically, it was shown how a spreadsheet can be used to develop a model by providing the modeller with an environment in which formulae can be developed both quickly and accurately. In doing so, the concept of formal spreadsheet modelling has been introduced. Moreover, the advantages of modelling a problem as well as a number of obvious shortcomings have been outlined. In particular, the advantage of building a model is that a greater understanding of a business problem can be afforded; coupled with the expertise and experience of the model user, this can facilitate effective decision-making. In contrast, the model user should be made aware that the model is only a simplification of reality and, as a consequence, the resultant output generated by a model represents only certain possible outcomes.

This book assumes that the reader has experience of basic spreadsheet operations and functions and is capable of building a small spreadsheet model. In this chapter a simple spreadsheet model has been considered and, for the reasons provided, it has been suggested that the resultant code is badly structured. In particular, the functional areas of data input, process and output overlap, and, by incorporating no on-screen help facilities, the model does not address the needs of the end user with limited spreadsheet knowledge.

At the end of the chapter, the concept of formal spreadsheet modelling was introduced. It has been demonstrated how this process encompasses a number of interrelated stages, which form the basis of this book. Additionally, the necessary features of any formal business model have been outlined, namely that it should be easy to use and maintain, be documented and cost-effective.

REVIEW QUESTIONS

1. Define the term 'model'.
2. What are the advantages and disadvantages of modelling a business problem?
3. What is the difference between a prescriptive model and a descriptive model? Give examples of both types of model which are different from those considered in this chapter.
4. Describe the following categories of model:
    – Analog
    – Iconic
    – Conceptual
    – Mathematical
5. List and describe *briefly* the essential features of a business model.
6. Describe the generic features of the spreadsheet.
7. Discuss *briefly* the advantages and disadvantages of exploiting the informality of the spreadsheet when developing a formal business model.
8. Describe the meaning of the term sequential when describing an approach to modelling. Outline the different stages in the (spreadsheet) modelling process.

9. Describe *briefly* why the modelling process is often iterative rather than sequential in nature.

10. Consider any spreadsheet model which you developed in the past. Do you consider this model to be user-friendly? (Ask someone to use it who has little or no spreadsheet experience.) Is the model badly structured? If so, describe what improvements could be made.

11. Using a pen and paper, sketch a more appropriate layout for this spreadsheet application. In your sketch include:
    - Functional sections of the model
    - On-screen help facilities that you would consider useful.

TWO

PROBLEM CONCEPTUALIZATION AND DATA ANALYSIS

OVERVIEW

This chapter describes those aspects of the modelling process which must be undertaken before any spreadsheet development takes place. This preliminary work consists of three stages: conceptualizing the problem under consideration, collecting the relevant data and examining the data collected. When describing data analysis, a brief description of how this may be undertaken using the facilities offered by Microsoft Excel will be provided.

OBJECTIVES

After reading this chapter and working through the questions, the reader will be able to:

- Understand the term 'problem conceptualization' and, for a given problem, be able to identify the model objective(s), the variables which need to be considered and the relationships that exist between these variables.
- Recognize the features of, and be able to construct, an influence diagram to depict the modelling situation.
- Recognize the benefits of using an influence diagram when building a conceptual model.
- Represent the relationships identified in the conceptual model using an influence diagram.
- Understand the term 'data analysis'.
- Recognize the existence of a number of powerful built-in facilities offered by Excel which can be used to display and examine a data set.

INTRODUCTION

While many model users have recognized the benefits of building and using formal spreadsheet models, some may not have fully understood the need to adopt a formal approach to model development. Because the spreadsheet provides an informal modelling environment, many modellers have a tendency to start programming immediately. However, there are three important steps which should be taken before any model development is undertaken:

- *Formulation of the modelling problem.* Problem formulation involves determining a model's objective(s), identifying the variables which need to be considered and determining the relationships that exist between these variables.

- *Collection of the (numerical) data*, paying attention to its relevance and accuracy.
- *Examination of the data set collected.* This examination may be undertaken using the spreadsheet and could perhaps include the creation of appropriate graphs and summary statistics. Moreover, initial (graphical or tabular) presentation and examination of the data collected may provide an early indication of the likely effectiveness of any formal model.

The steps described above form the basis of this chapter. One important feature of the steps outlined is that the three stages are both iterative and interrelated. That is, conceptualization of a problem involves building a 'paper' or diagrammatical model in which variables and relationships are identified. The size and complexity of the diagrammatical model will influence the size and content of the data set to be collected. The availability of relevant and accurate information may affect the complexity of the relationships which can be analysed, and, as a result, the conceptual model may have to be either altered or simplified. Finally, examination of the data set collected will give an indication of the validity of the conceptual model. As a consequence, modification of the conceptual model may have to take place, perhaps resulting in the collection and examination of additional data (hence demonstrating the iterative nature of the process). Only by undertaking these important steps (and repeating parts of the process if necessary) can the conceptual model be considered valid and representative.

THE SIMPLE MODELLING SCENARIO (the 'contractor's' problem)

To describe the three preliminary stages in developing a model, a simple modelling situation is referred to. The problem concerns the manager of a commercial decorating company (as introduced in Chapter 1) who wishes to predict the duration and cost of future contracts.

In this model, assume that each contract undertaken will involve buildings of a simple rectangular structure, comprising two long walls and two short walls. In practice, there may be contracts which involve decorating buildings of irregular shape. However, by assuming that each building has a simple structure, the formulae considered in the resultant model will be easy to construct and understand.

In this simple model, assume that the long wall is of height H (feet) and length L, while the shorter wall is of height H and width W. The shape of these two walls is illustrated in Figure 2.1.

Once the area of the building has been determined, it is assumed that contract duration can be estimated, and in turn, the hourly rate charged for the contract can be decided. Using the estimate of contract duration and the corresponding hourly rate, contract cost can be calculated.

The advantage of considering a problem which includes only a few simple formulae is that the reader can focus clearly on the modelling principles being introduced, rather than the

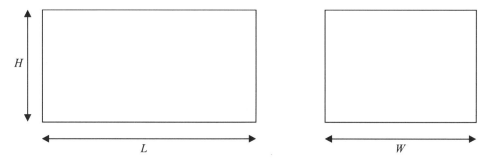

Figure 2.1 The dimensions of the building assumed in the 'contractor's' model

mathematics which underpin the model's calculations. The formulae which will be included in this formal model are described later in the chapter. In Chapters 2 to 7 inclusive, reference will be made to this simple modelling application, and the resultant spreadsheet program (written using Microsoft Excel) will be referred to as the 'contractor's' model. However, all of the underlying modelling principles which are introduced are readily applicable to more complex modelling situations and other spreadsheets.

Obviously not all of the features of the spreadsheet or all of the modelling principles will be used in the construction of an individual spreadsheet model. Where necessary, alternative business scenarios and models to illustrate the application of specific concepts or facilities will be considered.

PROBLEM CONCEPTUALIZATION

Problem conceptualization involves the modeller determining the decision(s) to be made, the variables which need to be considered, the behaviour of these variables and their interrelationships. Once these variables and relationships have been determined, they may be represented by a diagram on paper. By representing the problem situation as a diagram, the modeller is able to develop a representation of a problem which can be used effectively for communication with the model user. This representation is known as a conceptual model. The primary role of the conceptual model in the modelling process is to transform the problem situation into a mathematical model, which can be subsequently developed using the spreadsheet. The conceptual model is particularly useful because distinction can be made between input, process and output variables.

Moreover, the diagrammatical representation can provide an outline of the formal model's structure (i.e. it defines the model's input, manipulation of data and output) and it provides an effective method of communicating both the problem situation and the resultant spreadsheet model to the end user. A mathematical model (i.e. the model to be developed using the spreadsheet) will utilize numbers and formulae to represent the relationships between variables. For a model user with little mathematical or computing experience, a set of formulae is likely to be meaningless, and so will provide an ineffective method of communicating the features and assumptions which have been considered. Alternatively, a diagram can be used to display all the variables and relationships which will affect the decision(s) to be made, using English or written statements rather than mathematical labels.

When developing a conceptual model, there are a number of features to consider:

- Identifying the model's objectives
- Identifying the variables which need to be considered
- Determining the relationships that exist between the variables under consideration
- Quantifying the relationships between these variables

In the 'contractor's' problem, the objective is to determine the cost and duration of a future contract. The variables to be considered include the dimensions of a building (length, width, height, the number of doors and windows). Using this information, another variable may be determined, namely the building's area. Additionally, the function of the building, its quality and the experience of the contract staff employed may also be considered. These variables, along with the building's size (area), may be used to estimate the duration of a future contract. Finally, the cost of the contract is dependent not only on the estimated duration but on the hourly rate charged. In conclusion, the relationships identified in this simple model are:

$$\text{Area} = f\,(\text{Height, Width, Length, Doors, Windows})$$
$$\text{Duration} = f\,(\text{Area, Quality, Function, Staff})$$
$$\text{Hourly rate} = f\,(\text{Duration})$$
$$\text{Cost} = f\,(\text{Duration, Hourly rate})$$

where $A = f\,(B)$ means 'A is a function of B' (i.e. A is dependent upon or influenced by B).

Now that the relationships have been identified, they can be quantified using mathematical formulae. The formulae to be used in the resultant spreadsheet model will be formally introduced later in the chapter.

In general, identification of the variables and the interrelationships that exist is an essential part of the modelling process. In more complex modelling situations, a number of relationships may not be identified if a conceptual or diagrammatical model is not developed prior to spreadsheet development. As a consequence, the resultant spreadsheet model may prove unrepresentative of the situation it is supposed to represent. We shall now demonstrate how a conceptual model can be built to represent the simple modelling situation introduced in this chapter, given that the model's objective(s) and variables have been identified. Once the conceptual model has been developed, the modeller can use the diagram as a communication tool and the end user will be able to determine if the proposed model truly represents the problem under consideration. Once agreement has been reached between modeller and end user regarding the accuracy of the conceptual model, the relevant data can be collected and the assumptions included in the paper model can be tested. Data collection and analysis will be described in this chapter, again with reference to the simple 'contractor's' problem.

INFLUENCE DIAGRAMS

Once the model's objective and the corresponding variables have been defined, an appropriate 'paper' model can be developed. For the simple model under consideration, the relationships identified are:

$$\text{Area} = f\,(\text{Height, Width, Length, Doors, Windows})$$
$$\text{Duration} = f\,(\text{Area, Quality, Function, Staff})$$
$$\text{Hourly rate} = f\,(\text{Duration})$$
$$\text{Cost} = f\,(\text{Duration, Hourly rate})$$

and the output variables are contract duration and cost.

Obviously, the formulae listed provide a poor (and for some model users a difficult) way of communicating the relationships identified in the problem. This is particularly true for those model users with little or no training in manipulating algebra and mathematical formulae.

In order to counter these problems, it would be useful to apply tools to represent the end user's interpretation of the modelling situation. Moreover, by using such tools to represent the problem situation, it would be equally desirable if they led directly to the development of the required spreadsheet code which would be used eventually to represent the problem situation.

There are a number of different techniques which can be used to build a conceptual model. In this chapter, one technique will be described in detail, namely the *influence diagram*.

This diagram provides a useful modelling tool because symbols and lines are used to represent the variables and their interrelationships rather than mathematical formulae. Moreover, the influence diagram will include each variable identified in the modelling process and the type of relationship that exists between them will be denoted by a set of distinct symbols (to be defined shortly). In terms of the formal spreadsheet model, three specific types of variable must be identified, which in turn will be distinctly represented by the diagram. These are:

- Input variables
- Process variables
- Output variables

As the name suggests, an influence diagram displays diagrammatically what influence each variable has on each of the other variables identified in the problem situation. In other words, the term 'variable y influences variable z' means that the behaviour or value of variable z is influenced by the behaviour or value of variable y. For end users with little modelling experience, the conceptual model must be easy to read and understand, and in turn it must also accurately represent the end user's understanding of the problem situation. The influence diagram represents one way of representing the end user's understanding of the modelling process and can be used to convert this interpretation into a user-friendly model structure which incorporates the necessary formulae and data processes.

This chapter will demonstrate how the influence diagram is particularly useful because it can display all of the decisions which need to be made, in addition to distinguishing between the input, process and output variables which have been identified. Moreover, the relationships that exist between variables (i.e. which variables influence each other) can be incorporated in the diagram. In the contract example, the aim of the influence diagram is to illustrate by diagram which variables influence contract duration and cost. These two variables represent the output or decision variables for the problem, and therefore are of greatest interest to the model user. To represent this problem using an influence diagram, symbols as displayed in Figure 2.2 will be used.

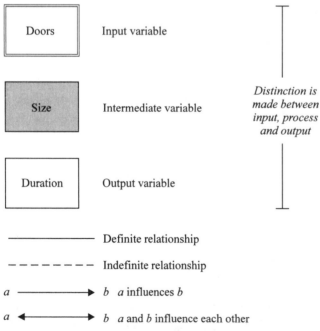

Figure 2.2   Symbols used in the influence diagram

In the influence diagram, distinction will be made between three different types of variable: input variables, intermediate (or process) variables and output variables.

Input variables

These are variables which can be either measured or controlled by the model user and represent the model's input parameters. Moreover, the value of these variables will change between contracts and, as a consequence, they will have to be measured/recorded before any (spreadsheet) model can be used to estimate contract cost.

In the 'contractor's' problem, the input variables are the building's dimensions, i.e. height, width, length, plus the number of doors and windows. Additionally, the quality of the building, the staff used on a particular contract and the building's function also represent input variables, because each of these vary according to an individual contract and so may influence contract duration and, in turn, contract cost.

Intermediate (or process) variables

Intermediate variables are those which are calculated (directly or indirectly) from the input variables but do not represent the model's output. An intermediate variable will in turn, influence (directly or indirectly) one or more of the decision variables. The 'contractor's' problem includes two intermediate variables: the building area (size) which is influenced by the building's dimensions (input variables) and the hourly rate charged for the particular contract.

Output variables

The output variables are those variables which will be used in the decision-making process. In the 'contractor's' problem, two output variables have been identified, namely the duration and cost of a particular contract.

REPRESENTING THE RELATIONSHIPS IN A CONCEPTUAL MODEL

So far, distinction has been made between input, intermediate and output variables, and indication has been given that certain variables in the problem situation may be related. In practice, the relationship between two variables may be definite or indefinite.

A number of the relationships identified in the modelling process may be definite, e.g. building height definitely influences area, and as a consequence such a relationship may be depicted accurately using a mathematical formula. In contrast, other relationships are more difficult to quantify and their influence can be described as indefinite. An example of an indefinite relationship in the 'contractor's' problem is the effect of a building's function on contract duration. For example, it may be reasonable to assume that a shop may take longer to paint than an office, but in practice this difference may be difficult or impossible to quantify. In the conceptual model it is useful to distinguish between definite and indefinite relationships. From the point of view of the modeller, areas of the model which may be potentially difficult to quantify can be identified, and in turn, by identifying these relationships, both modeller and model user will be aware of any potential shortcomings of the model. Moreover, the conceptual model may have to be simplified, but only after agreement between the two parties.

Figure 2.2 shows how relationships are represented within the influence diagram. In short, a line is used on the diagram to join the two boxes which represent the related variables. The direction of the arrow indicates the influence that exists. Moreover, it should be apparent that in certain cases one variable may influence another, or alternatively both variables influence each other.

Equally, it is useful to distinguish between definite and indefinite relationships. This has been achieved in this chapter by using two distinct symbols: a straight, continuous line to represent a definite relationship and a dotted line to represent an indefinite one.

If a large model is to be developed, it is unwise to build the conceptual model in one step. Instead, it is preferable to split the problem into small, self-contained parts and build the influence diagram section by section. In the 'contractor's' example, the small, self-contained subsets of the problem may be:

- The influence of building dimensions on area
- The influence of building attributes on contract duration
- The influence of contract duration and hourly rate on cost

In the next part of the chapter, an influence diagram will be built section by section to represent the 'contractor's' problem.

The influence of building dimensions on area

Figure 2.3 illustrates two ways of displaying the first subset of the influence diagram. This subset shows how the building's dimensions influence its size. Each input variable influences size definitely, but none of the input variables influence each other (i.e. no lines of influence join the input variables). Moreover, size is considered to be an intermediate variable, i.e. it does not represent part of the model's output, and as a consequence has been represented by an appropriate type of box.

In Figure 2.3, clear names have been given to the variables under consideration. That is, terms such as dimensions, height and area have been used and, as a consequence, the diagram provides the end user with information such as *height definitely influences building area*. In short, the influence diagram provides a simple but powerful communication tool, containing no ambiguous information.

By comparing the two diagrams presented in Figure 2.3, it should be obvious that the influence diagram can, when appropriate, be amplified to provide more detailed information. For example, the first diagram indicates that dimensions influence area, but, by splitting the dimension variable, the second diagram indicates that dimension is made up of height, width, length, doors and windows. In general, the diagram permits any variable to be split into smaller, simpler ones which may be used within the influence diagram. The use of a simple diagram or its more detailed equivalent will vary between modelling applications, and be dictated by both modeller and end user requirements.

The influence of building attributes on contract duration

The next section of the conceptual model indicates which variables influence contract duration. After discussions with the end user, the modeller may determine that the following factors are likely to influence the duration of a contract:

- *Size of the building*, i.e. its area.
- *Quality of the building*, i.e. if the building is old, new, damp, or in a state of disrepair.

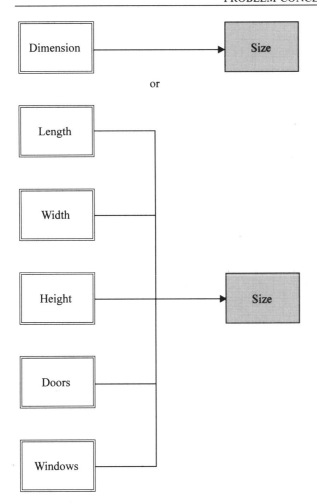

Figure 2.3 Influence diagrams illustrating how the building's dimensions influence building size

- *Personnel employed*, i.e. whether the staff undertaking a particular contract are trainees, qualified staff or a mix of personnel. Additionally, any labour disputes or stoppages may be considered.
- *Function of the building*, i.e. whether it is used as a shop, an office or an industrial unit. In turn, the building's function may influence its quality, i.e. an industrial unit may be subject to more wear and tear than an office or shop.

Before undertaking any decorating contract, it is likely that an inspection of the building may take place. At an inspection, the building's dimensions (length, width, height, windows and doors) can be measured accurately and the building area calculated. Additionally, the quality of the building may be assessed. Whereas the relationship between building size and duration is definite, an assessment of a building's quality may be subjective, and, as a result, may not be consistent with the inspections that have taken place at other buildings. It is also unlikely that the personnel who will carry out the contract will be known to the end user when using the

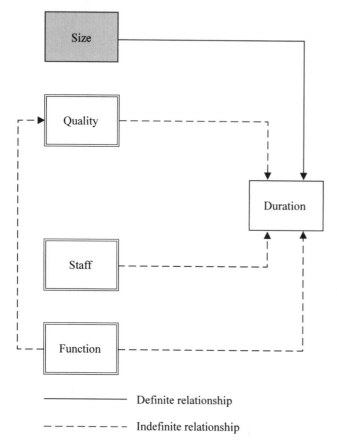

—————————— Definite relationship

— — — — — — — Indefinite relationship

Figure 2.4 Subset of the influence diagram concerning contract duration

model to predict duration. In short, the influence of quality and personnel on contract duration will be indefinite. Similarly, the impact of the building's function on contract duration is unpredictable, as described earlier in the chapter. For example, the time taken to decorate a retail outlet may not be significantly different from the time taken to decorate an office, and, as a consequence, the influence is indefinite.

Therefore, we have only one variable which definitely influences a contract's duration, i.e. a building's size. From past records, it may be possible to quantify a relationship between contract size and duration, and an approach which may be taken will be considered later in the chapter. Figure 2.4 illustrates how the variables described above influence contract duration.

It should be apparent that this section of the conceptual model indicates areas of potential weakness in the resultant spreadsheet program. In other words, the estimation of contract duration is influenced only definitely by one variable, and as a consequence the estimate made by using the model may or may not prove sufficiently accurate.

The influence of duration and hourly rate on cost

The second output variable to consider is contract cost. The cost of the contract is influenced (definitely) by two factors, namely contract duration and rate per hour. However, the decorating company offers different rates for contracts of varying duration. The hourly rates and corresponding contract durations are shown in Figure 2.5. As a consequence, contract duration definitely influences the hourly rate charged by the company as well as definitely influencing the total contract cost. Figure 2.6 illustrates the relationships between these variables.

The hourly rate charged for a particular contract is represented as an intermediate variable in the conceptual model. Hourly rate is labelled in this way because it is influenced by other variables in the model, but at the same time does not (explicitly) represent part of the model's output.

Influence diagrams have now been developed to depict each of the separate self-contained parts of the problem and have been shown in Figures 2.3, 2.4 and 2.6. Once agreement has been reached between modeller and model user regarding their completeness, logic and accuracy, they can be combined to provide the influence diagram which represents the whole modelling process. The influence diagram representing the whole of the contract problem is shown in Figure 2.7.

The completed influence diagram represents a tool for communication between modeller and model user. Once the latter agrees with the information presented in the completed influence diagram, analysis can be undertaken to determine the exact character of each relationship identified. When the relationships have been measured, quantified or estimated, the relevant spreadsheet code can be developed.

Moreover, it should also be apparent that the problem has been represented completely and accurately using a set of symbols within a simple structure and the level of detail provided in this diagram can be either increased or decreased depending upon the needs of the model user.

Hourly rate (£)	Contract duration (hours)
12.75	0 −
11.50	10 −
10.85	20 −
9.75	30 −
9.50	40 −
9.00	50 −
8.00	100 +

Figure 2.5 Hourly rates charged by the company

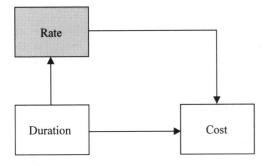

Figure 2.6 Influence diagram for contract cost

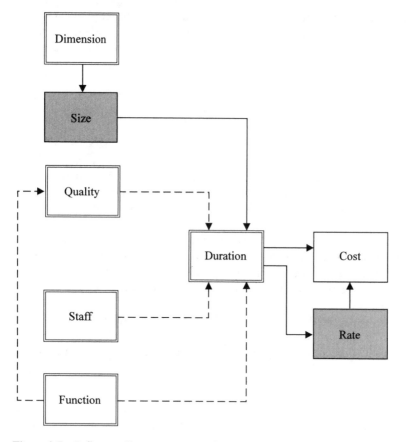

Figure 2.7 Influence diagram representing the 'contractor's' problem

In conclusion, the influence diagram is a useful modelling tool because:

- Distinction is made between input, intermediate (process) and output variables
- Distinction is made between definite and indefinite relationships, and, as a consequence, areas of potential weakness in the modelling process can be identified
- Symbols are used to represent the different types of variable and relationship, thus providing greater understanding and communication than can ever be provided by a list of equations or mathematical formulae

Moreover, the influence diagram can be used to its full potential if the problem under consideration is split into smaller, related parts. An influence diagram can be used to represent each part of the whole problem and, once agreement is reached on the completeness and accuracy, these can be combined in the appropriate way to represent the whole problem.

In order to maximize its potential as a communication tool, the influence diagram should use clear, unambiguous names to represent each variable identified in the problem. Moreover, by splitting certain variables into smaller ones, more detailed information can be provided, i.e. height, width, length, doors and windows are used instead of dimensions in the influence diagram representing the 'contractor's' problem.

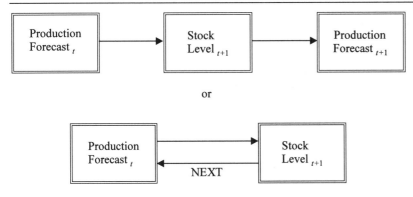

Figure 2.8 Influence diagram showing variables related over time

There may also be occasions when an influence diagram is used to demonstrate the relationship between two variables over time. A small company which produces parts for the computer industry may forecast levels of production in its factory. Production forecasts for time t will influence the level of stock at time $t + 1$, which in turn will influence the next production forecast. Figure 2.8 shows two possible ways of demonstrating this relationship using an influence diagram.

Notice that the first influence diagram in Figure 2.8 does not contain a loop between Production Forecast and Stock Level because the successive forecasts are two separate variables. If a large number of forecasts are to be made (say weekly instead of annually), the influence diagram will soon grow large and, unfortunately, will diminish as a tool for communication between modeller and model user. However, if subscripts are used in the boxes and labels on the arrows to denote the exact nature of the relationships, the influence diagram can be greatly simplified. In the lower diagram in Figure 2.8, the influence diagram suggests that Production Forecast$_t$ influences Stock Level$_{t+1}$ and this is shown by the direction of the top arrow. The bottom arrow carries the label 'NEXT' to indicate that Stock Level$_{t+1}$ influences the next forecast, i.e. Production Forecast$_{t+1}$. Even at this stage the diagram has shown a degree of simplification. In the same way, the term 'PREVIOUS' can be used as a label on the influence diagram arrow where appropriate. Moreover, it may be useful to add additional comments to the influence diagram indicating the likely values of t. If forecasts are to be made weekly over the course of a year in the product example, the statement $t = 1, 52$ could be added to the diagram (Figure 2.8).

Now that the conceptual model has been developed, the next stage to be undertaken in the modelling process involves the examination of the relationships assumed and represented by the influence diagram. This examination consists of two stages: collection of relevant information and analysis of the data collected. With reference to the simple problem, these issues are described in the following sections of the chapter. Once this analysis has been undertaken, examination of the detail included in the influence diagram can be amended as required.

DATA COLLECTION

To construct any formal model, the modeller must collect an accurate set of data which is representative of the subject of interest. The data set can be collected either from the whole of the population of interest (i.e. by considering all of the contracts undertaken by the company), in which case a *census* would be undertaken, or from part of the population, in which case a *sample* of data is collected.

Obviously, the most accurate data set may be obtained by considering all previous contracts, but this may be impractical because of the volume of data involved or lack of relevant information. Moreover, the modeller should be aware of the trade-off between the volume of data collected and the accuracy of any subsequent analysis with the cost (time and money) of data collection. However, if a sample or subset of data is to be used, it must be representative of the subject of interest in order to maximize the effectiveness of any resultant (spreadsheet) model. It would also be useful (if possible) for the modeller to determine the accuracy of any data recorded for a particular contract, i.e. if exact measurements of contract duration and building area were made or estimates taken instead. In other modelling situations, it is useful to determine if the data collected represents exact values or whether processes such as averaging or rounding have taken place. Using estimated values or data which have undergone a range of processes or simplifications may affect the relationships determined by the modeller.

In general, the larger the data set collected by the modeller, the more accurate and representative the model is likely to be. In practice, the volume of data collected will be determined by three factors:

- The level of model accuracy required by the end user
- The cost of data collection
- The time available before decisions need to be made

In the 'contractor's' problem, a sample of data is required so that the modeller may determine accurately the relationship between duration (and cost) and contract attributes such as building size, quality and function. Additionally, the modeller may wish to determine the influence of personnel employed on contract duration. Inspection of the company's records will indicate the availability of the required information. When attempting to collect the relevant information, the modeller may find that while data is available regarding contract duration and size, no information has been recorded about the building's function and quality or the staff employed on each particular contract. As a consequence, the influence diagram built to represent the 'contractor's' problem and agreed both by the modeller and end user must be simplified. The revised (simplified) conceptual model is illustrated in Figure 2.9.

To quantify the relationship between building size and contract duration, a sample of ten recent contracts has been selected. After discussion with the contracts manager (the model user), the modeller will assume that the data set is representative of the work undertaken by the company. Figure 2.10 lists the data set. Now that a representative data set has been collected, data analysis can be undertaken to determine the nature of the relationship between building size and contract duration.

DATA ANALYSIS

Data analysis is the term given to the process of examining a data set using appropriate statistical and graphical techniques. In short, the examination of a data set consists of four main stages:

- Presenting the data in a way which will facilitate analysis. Many modern spreadsheets incorporate *database* facilities which may be used to store relevant numerical information. The

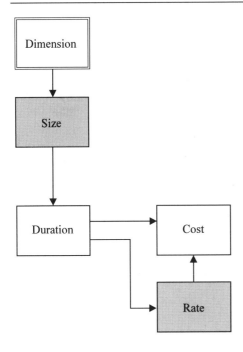

Figure 2.9 The updated (and simplified) conceptual model

Area (sq. feet)	*Time* (hours)
250	8.75
326	11.25
275	9.88
387	15.56
450	21.87
224	12.50
356	16.50
442	21.35
280	15.77
210	7.67

Figure 2.10 A sample of contracts undertaken by the company

facilities provided usually include *sort*, *search* and *extract* routines, which can be used if necessary to simplify or enhance the presentation of the data collected.
- Inspection of each variable in the data set for validity and property. Inspection for validity and property will involve identifying extreme observations and missing information. In particular, the creation of frequency distributions (graphical or tabular) for each variable is a useful way of determining their individual properties.
- The creation of appropriate summary statistics and graphs. In particular, producing a scatter graph to identify the character of a relationship between two variables will help to test any assumptions made during the development of the conceptual model. A scatter graph can be

used in the 'contractor's' problem to identify the strength and nature of the relationship between building size and contract duration.

• Assessing the viability of developing a formal model.

In the 'contractor's' problem, the modeller needs to determine the behaviour of the input and intermediate variables identified by the conceptual model. Specifically, the modeller must determine the nature and strength of the relationship between contract duration and building area. By undertaking this analysis, the validity of the conceptual model can be assessed and, if necessary, further modifications can take place.

A number of numerical tests can be undertaken using the facilities offered by the spreadsheet. The next part of the chapter considers two important spreadsheet facilities, namely:

• The generation of summary statistics
• The construction of suitable graphs and scatter diagrams

By considering these facilities, it is assumed that the modeller will be aware of the availability and properties of the relevant functions within their own spreadsheet. As a consequence, the level of functional detail will be kept to a minimum, although details of the functional provision within Excel is provided.

Statistical functions

When analysing a data set, the modeller may wish to calculate summary statistics for each of the variables under consideration. In Excel, there are a number of built-in statistical commands which can be utilized, for example:

AVERAGE()   (calculates the *average* value of a data set)
STDEV()   (calculates the *standard deviation*)
STDEVP()
VAR()   (calculates the *variance*)
SUM()   (calculates the *total*)
COUNT()   (counts the number of *observations* in a data set)
MAX()   (calculates the *maximum*)
MIN()   (calculates the *minimum*)
MEDIAN()   (calculates the *median*)
MODE()   (calculates the *mode*)

Moreover, Excel also provides a sophisticated statistical toolkit which includes the functions listed above as well as a wide range of other statistical tools. In particular, the Excel toolkit includes the following facilities:

Anova
Correlation
Covariance
Descriptive statistics *(lists those statistics provided by the functions above)*
Exponential smoothing
F test
Histogram
Moving average
Rank and percentile

Regression

t test and z test

After a data set is entered into the Excel spreadsheet, the toolkit may be activated by selecting:

<u>O</u>ptions
<u>A</u>nalysis Tools

Figure 2.11 shows the toolkit window, which indicates that the Descriptive Statistics facility has been selected, the window corresponding to the selected facility and the output generated.

Tabular and graphical presentation of data

In addition to generating summary statistics, the modeller may wish to examine the distribution of the individual variables in a data set by generating frequency distribution tables and graphs. In Excel, a frequency distribution table can be generated using the Histogram facility offered as part of the spreadsheet's toolkit. Once a frequency distribution table has been constructed for a particular variable using this function, a graphical display (i.e. a histogram) is generated automatically by Excel.

Additionally, the modeller may need to determine what relationships exist, if any, between pairs of variables identified by the conceptual model. In the 'contractor's' problem, the conceptual model highlighted that a definite relationship is likely to exist between contract duration and building area (i.e. area *definitely influences* duration). To verify this relationship, a representative set of data has been collected, as shown in Figure 2.10. The relationship suggested by the influence diagram can be verified by constructing a scatter diagram using the ChartWizard facility offered by Excel. The scatter diagram generated for the contract data is shown in Figure 2.13, and, as suggested, this shows that building area definitely influences contract duration.

To develop a graph using this facility, the modeller must highlight the data to be graphed, and click the ChartWizard icon:

After activating the ChartWizard facility, the modeller needs to define the graph area by dragging on the mouse. The graph can then be built by simply following the menu facility offered by ChartWizard. This menu is illustrated by Figure 2.12 and the resultant scatter diagram is shown in Figure 2.13.

The scatter diagram shown in Figure 2.13 supports the assumption made during the development of the conceptual model. Moreover, it would appear that duration can be accurately estimated from contract size, and, as a result, this suggests that any formal spreadsheet model would provide reasonably accurate predictions of contract duration.

In general, data analysis enables the modeller to assess the benefits of developing a formal model at an early stage. In many situations, verification of the relationships between variables and the examination of the distribution of individual variables identified by the conceptual model may provide sufficient information for the end user. Alternatively, the results may provide the necessary indication that the conceptual model of the problem situation is valid and that construction of the spreadsheet model may commence. Finally, the process of data examination may highlight that certain variables are badly behaved or that expected relationships between variables are either weak or non-existent. As a result, the conceptual model may have to be amended, while in extreme situations there may be little achieved in building a formal

Analysis Tools

Anova: Single-Factor
Anova: Two-Factor With Replication
Anova: Two-Factor Without Replication
Correlation
Covariance
Descriptive Statistics
Exponential Smoothing
F-Test: Two-Sample for Variances

OK
Cancel
Help

Descriptive Statistics

Input Range: $B$5:$B$14

Output Range:

Grouped By: ● **Columns**
                  ○ **Rows**

☐ **Labels In First Row**   ☒ **Summary Statistics**
☐ **Kth Largest:** 1
☐ **Kth Smallest:** 1
☐ **Confidence Level for Mean:** 95   %

OK
Cancel
Help

	A	B
29		
30	*Column 1*	
31		
32	Mean	14.06
33	Standard Error	1.563146
34	Median	14.03
35	Mode	#N/A
36	Standard Deviation	4.943101
37	Variance	24.43424
38	Kurtosis	-0.89989
39	Skewness	0.425264
40	Range	14.2
41	Minimum	7.67
42	Maximum	21.87
43	Sum	140.6
44	Count	10

Figure 2.11   Generating summary statistics using Excel's toolkit

business model. If the modeller decides that it is impractical to build a formal model, time will have been saved by undertaking data analysis and so any unnecessary expense will not be incurred.

DERIVING THE FORMULAE TO BE INCLUDED IN THE MODEL

Once the data analysis has been undertaken and both modeller and model user are reasonably confident that the conceptual model is complete and sufficiently accurate, the modeller needs to determine the calculations and process which must be included in the spreadsheet model. From the influence diagram (conceptual model) representing the 'contractor's' problem, four calculations need to be included in the spreadsheet model.

1. Calculation of building size

In this simple model, assume that the long wall is of height H (feet) and length L, while the shorter wall is of height H and width W. The shape of these two walls was illustrated in Figure 2.1.

Assuming a simple four-wall building:

Area of the 'long' wall = LENGTH * HEIGHT

Area of the 'short' wall = WIDTH * HEIGHT

Total area = 2 * (LENGTH * HEIGHT + WIDTH * HEIGHT)

= 2 * HEIGHT * (LENGTH + WIDTH)

If the standard areas of the doors and windows are 21 and 15 square feet respectively, then

Total area of the doors in the building = 21 * DOORS

Total area of the windows in the building = 15 * WINDOWS

Therefore, the required formula for the area to be painted is:

Area = 2 * HEIGHT * (LENGTH + WIDTH) − ((21 * DOORS) + (15 * WINDOWS))

As indicated by the influence diagram, a definite relationship exists between building area and each of the building's dimensions. This relationship has now been quantified exactly by formula.

2. Determining the relationship between contract size and duration

It has been indicated from the scatter diagram in Figure 2.13 that a positive linear relationship exists between these two variables, i.e. as building area increases, contract duration increases. As a consequence, the relationship can be represented by the least squares regression line:

$$y = a + bx$$

where y represents contract duration and x represents building size.

Since the modeller is using Microsoft Excel, the necessary output can be generated using the **INTERCEPT( )** and **SLOPE( )** commands for small data sets or by using the regression output incorporated in the spreadsheet's toolkit. In general, inspection of an individual spreadsheet by the modeller will indicate the existence of specific built-in commands. However, whenever built-in functions are to be used, the modeller should ensure that the built-in facility operates exactly

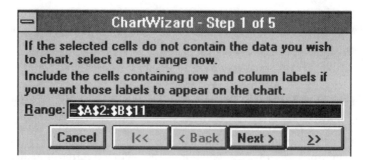

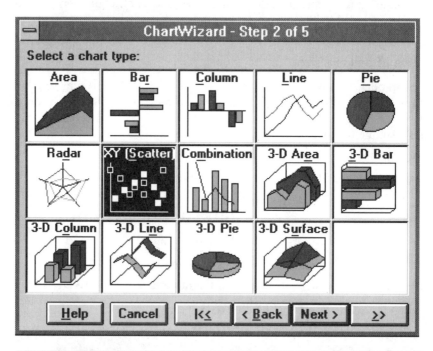

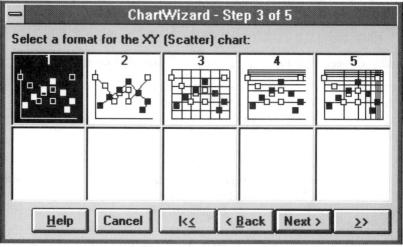

Figure 2.12 The ChartWizard facility offered by Excel

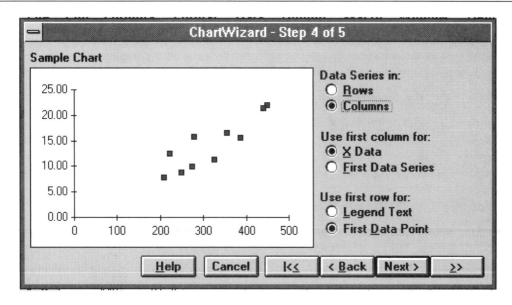

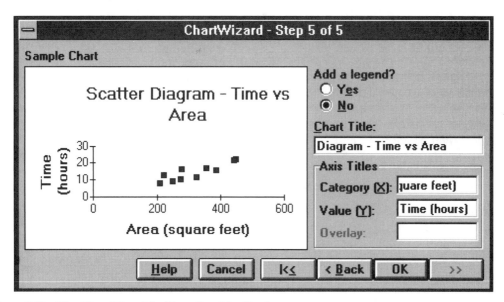

Figure 2.12   The ChartWizard facility offered by Excel

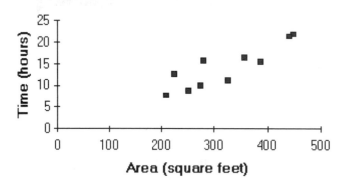

Figure 2.13   Scatter diagram showing the relationship between contract size and duration

as required. Potential problems which may be encountered when using built-in functions are described by reference to specific Excel facilities in Chapter 4.

3. Selecting the appropriate hourly rate

Hourly rate is influenced by contract duration, and the different rates charged by the company are listed in Figure 2.5. Excel provides a function (**VLOOKUP( )**) which can be used to select appropriate values from a table of data, and, as a result, dependent calculations can be greatly simplified. The role of this Excel function will described in Chapter 4.

4. Calculation of contract cost

Cost can be calculated using the equation:

$$\text{Cost}(\pounds) = \text{Estimated duration (hour)} \times \text{Hourly rate (£/hour)}$$

The simple formula listed above can be translated easily into spreadsheet code. Before any coding is undertaken, the modeller should produce a detailed paper-based map which will be used to define the layout of the spreadsheet model. If the model is being developed for an end user with limited spreadsheet experience, this map should consist of two main parts:

- *User support facilities* (introduction, help, on-screen map)
- *Functional sections of the model* (input, processes and output)

In particular, the 'contractor's' model will have three main functional areas:

- An *input* routine which handles the entry of the model's parameters (dimensions) for a particular contract, i.e. height, width, length, plus the number of doors and windows
- A *process* routine which deals with the calculation of contract size and duration, identification of the appropriate hourly rate and the calculation of contract cost
- An *output* routine which displays a contract's duration and cost

The paper-based map may resemble the diagram in Figure 2.14. The map consists of a number of separate, self-contained sections. The top set of sections in Figure 2.14 deals with user support, while the bottom sections house the functional areas of the model. It should be

Introduction	Help	On-screen map
Input - Height - Width - Length - Doors - Windows	**Process** - Area - Hourly rates	**Output** - Duration - Cost

Figure 2.14 A paper-based model map

apparent that the structure outlined by this map is more user-friendly and responsive to change than the structure depicted previously by Figure 1.2. The role of the specific areas labelled on the map will be described in detail with reference to the 'contractor's' problem in Chapter 4.

The conceptual model represented by the influence diagram in Figure 2.9 will prove particularly useful when designing this map because distinction has been made between the variables which belong to the separate functional areas of data input, process and output. Specifically, these areas have been kept separate and self-contained on the model map. Moreover, if a modelling template (i.e. a skeleton model structure based on the separate, self-contained areas shown in Figure 2.14 – see Chapter 10 for more details on model templates) is to be used, cell references for each block (and perhaps also for each variable and calculation) can also be added to the paper-based spreadsheet map.

In conclusion, at the start of the chapter an unstructured business problem was introduced. This has been represented diagrammatically using an influence diagram. Because this diagram contains symbols and lines to represent each variable and their interrelationships rather than mathematical formulae, the end user can determine quickly if the business problem has been properly represented. Once agreement has been reached between modeller and model user, the assumptions included on the diagram can be tested and the modeller will be in a position to determine the size of the resultant spreadsheet model. Once this has been achieved, a paper-based model map can be drawn. The influence diagram also plays its part in the addition of detail to this map, because distinction has been made between the input, process and output variables.

CONCLUSIONS

In this chapter, the necessary steps to be taken prior to the development of a formal (spreadsheet) model have been described. This preliminary work consists of three stages:

- Conceptualizing the modelling situation
- Collecting the relevant data
- Examining the data collected

In problem conceptualization, formulating the modelling situation involves identifying objectives and constraints as well as identifying the relationships that may exist between variables. Once these areas have been identified, a particular diagram can be used to represent the variables considered in the problem and their interrelationships. This representation is known as an *influence diagram.*

Once a business problem has been described diagrammatically and the relationships between variables identified, the modeller can verify the existence of each relationship. There are a number of spreadsheet facilities which may be utilized when measuring these relationships: in particular, summary statistics and graphs. Moreover, the results of this analysis will help determine the validity of the conceptual model (described earlier in this chapter) and, in turn, this analysis will provide an indication of the likely effectiveness of the formal spreadsheet model. Alternatively, the analysis undertaken may prove sufficiently useful in a number of situations to permit the model user to take the correct course of action.

Once the conceptual model has been validated, the modeller will be aware of the input, process and output requirements of the subsequent spreadsheet model. By referring to the influence diagram, a paper-based map can be developed, specifically keeping the functional areas of data input, process and output separate and self-contained. If the paper map is based on a modelling template, additional detail such as cell references for each self-contained block and each variable/calculation may be added. Moreover, this map can be subsequently used as a blueprint for the actual spreadsheet model.

REVIEW QUESTIONS

1. Define the term 'problem conceptualization'.
2. What steps should be undertaken when conceptualizing a problem?
3. What is an influence diagram? Describe the advantages of using an influence diagram during problem conceptualization.
4. Describe the different types of variable and relationships which may be considered in an influence diagram.
5. *A* and *B* represent input variables for a particular modelling situation. *C* represents an intermediate or process variable and *D* represents the model's output variable. Define the symbols which represent *A*, *B*, *C* and *D*. Given that *A* influences *C* definitely and *B* influences both *A* and *C* indefinitely, represent this information using an influence diagram. *C* definitely influences *D*. Represent this relationship using an influence diagram. Finally, combine both diagrams to represent the whole problem diagrammatically.
6. Define the term 'data analysis'.
7. Describe *briefly* the four stages of data analysis.
8. Why is an influence diagram a useful tool when developing a paper-based model map?
9. Consider the spreadsheet with which you are most familiar. Which of the following features are included?
   - Database
   - Graphs
   - Summary statistics
   - Regression analysis
   - Statistics toolkit
   Consider each available facility in detail, and learn how to apply them to a range of data sets.

CASE STUDY QUESTIONS

1. A small manufacturer wishes to invest in some new equipment. The cost of this investment is estimated to be £20 000. The new machinery is likely to result in the production of 10 000 units of a particular product, and the manufacturer expects all units to be sold. After the first year, unit sales are expected to fall by 5 per cent per annum, and after 5 years it can be assumed sales will be zero and the machinery obsolete. The manufacturer estimates the unit selling price to be £8 and unit costs to be £6.50. The current rate of interest charged by the bank to small business borrowers is 12 per cent. The manufacturer wishes to determine the viability of this investment and would like to develop a spreadsheet model to assist in the decision-making process. After consultation with the model user, it has been agreed that the net present value (NPV) method of investment appraisal will be used to assess the viability of the proposed purchase. It can be assumed that 60 per cent of sales revenue is received in the year that the sales are made, 30 per cent in the subsequent year and the remainder is never received. All costs are paid in the year of production.

    The first stage in the development of the spreadsheet model requires the creation of an *influence diagram* to depict the investment problem. On the influence diagram, distinction needs to be made between input, process and output variables, as well as definite and indefinite relationships.
2. Once the conceptual model has been constructed, derive the formulae that need to be included in the formal model.
3. List the *input*, *process* and *output* variables that should be included in the formal spreadsheet model.
4. Sketch a paper-based spreadsheet map, indicating the location of the variables listed as your answer to question 3. Do not spend too much time on this map, because alternative structures will be considered in the next chapter.

THREE

DESIGNING A FORMAL SPREADSHEET MODEL

OVERVIEW

This chapter describes structured methods of designing formal spreadsheet models. In particular, practical methods of model layout are demonstrated, paying attention to the efficient use of memory, which may prove critical in the development of a larger model. In describing a structured approach to model development, the chapter shows how the methods of layout described can ensure that the different sections of the model remain separate.

OBJECTIVES

After reading this chapter and working through the questions, the reader will be able to:

- Understand why a spreadsheet model needs to incorporate a formal structure
- Recognize the appropriate methods of structuring a spreadsheet model, especially when allocation of computer memory may prove critical
- Demonstrate how a formal model structure can ensure that different sections of a model remain separate

INTRODUCTION

While many business personnel utilize the spreadsheet to provide quick and accurate responses to business problems, many others have exploited the significant modelling enhancements available in a number of modern spreadsheets. Moreover, the concept of formal spreadsheet modelling has become widely accepted in many organizations. Because of the informal environment provided by the spreadsheet, many modellers may have built models in a piecemeal fashion paying little or no attention to model layout (see Figure 1.1). As a consequence, the resultant programs have been difficult to utilize and maintain. Perhaps the most common mistake made when developing a model in this way is that the areas of data input, process and output overlap, making the resultant code difficult to understand, especially for those model users with little computing experience.

In the early part of this chapter, three user-friendly model structures that may be used in the construction of a formal model are considered. The most important feature of the structures described is that the different sections of the model remain self-contained and separate, in particular those 'functional' areas listed in the previous paragraph. The importance of model structure is firstly emphasized by making a comparison with the structured (programming) techniques employed by computing professionals who work with high-level programming languages.

Once the issue of model structure has been addressed, in Chapter 4 the role and contents of each of the self-contained blocks contained within a formal, spreadsheet model are described in general terms. This is achieved by making reference to a simple but formal 'contractor's' model which has been developed using Microsoft Excel. The present chapter will list the features (in terms of a block structure) to be included in this simple model. The concepts introduced in this chapter are addressed in a general manner and, as a result, are readily applicable and transferable to other spreadsheets and modelling applications.

TOP-DOWN PROGRAM DESIGN FOR HIGH-LEVEL LANGUAGES

One accepted method of program design utilized by many professionals working with high-level languages is the 'top-down' method, which is particularly useful when writing large or complex programs. In adopting this method of program design, the programmer starts with a broad plan of the problem, written in English rather than program code. Detail is then incorporated into this general plan until coding becomes possible.

Figure 3.1 illustrates a general 'top-down' plan where the main program is linked to a number of subprograms, which *individually* handle the areas of data input, process (calculations) and output. In turn, these subprograms are self-contained and perform one specific function. Employing a subprogram for each individual routine ensures that the resultant code becomes easier to write, understand and maintain.

In the same way, each of the subprograms can be separated (if appropriate) into smaller and simpler programs. This is illustrated in Figure 3.2, where the subprogram which handles data

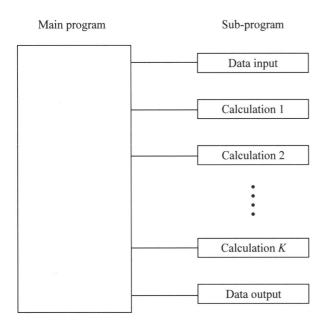

Figure 3.1 Top-down structure for a high-level program

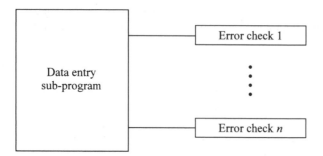

Figure 3.2 Top-down simplification of the data entry routine

input has been broken down into a number of smaller routines, each of which deals with the input of an *individual* variable. The most important benefit of utilizing this method of program design is that the resultant routines are easy to understand and maintain. Additionally, these routines can be written in such a way as to ensure the validity of each of the program's parameters. Moreover, at this stage of program development, the broad plan will contain a level of detail which will facilitate the creation of the required program code. Note that validation of a spreadsheet model's parameters is also an essential part of model development and is considered in detail in Chapter 6.

If a structured approach can be used when writing a computer program, why are spreadsheet models written for end users with limited computer experience developed in an untidy, piecemeal manner? Instead, an analogous structure will be proposed for the development of a formal spreadsheet model. Many modellers might take the view that such a proposal contradicts the principle of 'informal computing', which underpins the popularity of the spreadsheet. However, absence of a predetermined structure will lead to the development of a model which may be difficult to utilize, maintain and, in time, amend. A model which is difficult to use will cause problems for the end user, while a model which is awkward to maintain or amend will prove cumbersome for the modeller.

Additionally, the model structures described are chosen with regard both to end user and modeller friendliness and are designed primarily to ensure that the 'functional' areas of data input, process and output remain separate in an equivalent way to that demonstrated in Figure 3.1. Moreover, in models developed without regard to structure, a major source of end-user error is the input of data which overwrites the model's formulae and programming routines.

DESIGN OF A SPREADSHEET MODEL

There are a number of interrelated stages involved in the modelling process as a whole, which have been outlined in Chapter 1. Moreover, the complexity of any individual model is driven by the problem under consideration. One stage in this process is the design of the model structure and identification of the model's contents. In undertaking this stage of the modelling process, there are five main areas of consideration:

- Determining the suitability of the spreadsheet itself
- Planning the content of the model

- Designing the layout of the model, paying attention to memory allocation (if this is a critical factor) in the development of larger models
- Use of appropriate built-in functions and construction of formulae
- Model automation

For simplicity, these considerations can be assumed to be sequential. However, if a modeller is to use the same spreadsheet for a number of modelling applications, then the choice of model layout made with regard to memory allocation is likely to be the same for all modelling applications. This may allow the modeller to design a generic modelling template (i.e. a 'skeleton' model consisting of a structure and limited spreadsheet code) which can be utilized in the development of any future model. The design and application of modelling templates is addressed in Chapter 10.

DETERMINING THE SUITABILITY OF THE SPREADSHEET

Before developing a formal model, the modeller needs to decide whether the spreadsheet is the most appropriate software tool. If the modelling application is small and simplistic and the end user has little or no experience of spreadsheets, then an electronic calculator supported by comprehensive instructions may be more suitable. In contrast, a number of applications may require huge data input and calculations of a highly iterative nature. These are best tackled by utilizing the capabilities of a high-level programming language such as Pascal or Fortran. Additionally, a number of specific application packages may be available to the model user. These include statistical packages such as MINITAB and decision support software which deal with specific modelling applications such as linear and goal programming and critical path analysis.

However, many of the modern spreadsheets have considerable modelling capabilities afforded by the inclusion of a number of specific built-in facilities. Examples of such built-in facilities include the Regression function (described in Chapter 2) and powerful functions which enable a number of spreadsheets to be used as pseudo-programming languages. Moreover, for many business personnel, the spreadsheet may be either the only application software they are trained to use or the only modelling software available within their organization. Additionally, a large number of business personnel appreciate the informal environment provided by the spreadsheet. Because of these factors and the need to facilitate decision-making, the concept of formal spreadsheet modelling has been addressed within many organizations.

After identifying that the spreadsheet is a suitable type of software, the modeller should use the conceptual model (described in Chapter 2) to design a *paper-based spreadsheet map*. This map is a diagrammatical representation of the future model and should be used as a blueprint for any subsequent spreadsheet model. In its design, the modeller should take into account the size and nature of data entry, the contents and complexity of the data processes and its user-defined output specifications. Additionally, the modeller should be aware of the end-user requirements with respect to on-screen instructions and help facilities. User support facilities such as introductory screens, help facilities and spreadsheet maps (on-screen maps locating the different components of the model by cell reference) should also be incorporated into the prototype map. This initial (paper-based) map should play an integral part in the spreadsheet development and also in the subsequent documentation of the spreadsheet model. The role of mapping in model documentation is described in Chapter 7. Once this mapping process has been completed, then the spreadsheet development can begin.

PLANNING THE CONTENT OF THE MODEL

The structure of a formal spreadsheet model should be planned away from the PC and must precede any spreadsheet development. Specifically, the model's structure should be decided during the design of the spreadsheet map. Additionally, the mathematical relationships identified by the modeller and represented by the conceptual model should influence the manipulations of data and the calculations which need to be undertaken. In particular, the modeller can determine the suitability of any built-in functions offered by the spreadsheet, and whether ready-built (in-house) modelling templates ('skeleton' structure of a formal model) or custom-built bolt-on programs (specific models bought 'off the shelf') can be utilized. The suitability of templates and bolt-on programs is described in Chapter 10.

If a modeller chooses to utilize a built-in function offered by the spreadsheet, then rigorous testing must be undertaken to guarantee that the selected function operates in the required way. Moreover, if there is any difference between actual and expected output, then the modeller should ensure that any systematic difference can be accounted for by the model.

Even the simplest of functions should be tested by the modeller before using them in a formal spreadsheet model. For example, Microsoft Excel provides a function = **AVERAGE( )** which can be used to compute the arithmetic mean for a data set. However, if a data set contains blank cells (representing missing values rather than zeros), does the function operate in the way required by the modeller? Moreover, is the behaviour of this function different from that of equivalent functions offered by other spreadsheets? Excel also provides a function = **STDEVP( )** which computes the standard deviation of a data set. However, it is important to realize when using this simple function that the value calculated is a population standard deviation rather than a sample statistic (the sample standard deviation can be computed using = **STDEV( )** instead). In short, even the simpler built-in functions may prove problematic.

Figure 3.3 illustrates the use of another built-in facility provided by Microsoft Excel, namely the = **NPV( )** function which can be used to calculate the net present value of an investment. Net present value (NPV) is a method of investment appraisal which enables a future set of cashflows

	A	B	C	D	E	F	G	H	I
					NPV.XLS				
4									
5									
6		By calculation:							
7									
8				Net	Discount	Present			
9			Year	Cashflow	Factor	Value			
10			0	-3500	1.0000	-3500			
11			1	4750	0.9132	4338			
12			2	3500	0.8340	2919			
13			3	2975	0.7617	2266			
14			4	1500	0.6956	1043			
15			5	550	0.6352	349			
16									
17					NPV =	£7416			
18									
19		By built-in function:							
20					NPV =	£6772			
21									

Figure 3.3 Testing the logic of a built-in function

to be expressed in terms of their present money value. The net present value (NPV) represents the sum of these individual present values. The screen in Figure 3.3 shows two calculations of NPV for one particular investment, the first involving the computation of a project's present value by constructing of the necessary formulae on the spreadsheet, the second by utilizing the built-in = **NPV( )** facility.

In the example illustrated, the formulae constructed on the spreadsheet yield an NPV of £7416 compared with a net present value of £6772 generated by the spreadsheet's built-in facility. In utilizing the built-in function, the formula entered in cell F20 is:

$$= \textbf{NPV(D2, D10:D15)}$$

where D2 stated the discount factor and D10:D15 represents the range of cashflows.

In this example the difference in NPVs obtained can be explained by the fact that Excel assumes that the first cashflow in the defined range corresponds to year one of the project and *not* the present time (i.e. year zero). Fortunately for both modeller and model user, the features of both Excel's **NPV( )** and statistical functions are explained clearly and fully by the on-line help facility provided by the spreadsheet. The thoroughness of this help facility should be apparent to the modeller, and in most non-trivial modelling applications it is likely to prove very helpful.

In general, the documentation provided by the spreadsheet manufacturer should contain details about the underlying assumptions contained in each built-in facility. In practice, the level of detail provided will vary from spreadsheet to spreadsheet and perhaps from function to function within individual packages. Moreover, the behaviour of certain built-in functions may also vary from spreadsheet to spreadsheet (the function for calculating the arithmetic mean is arguably the simplest example, where Excel's average function ignores blank cells in array, while other spreadsheets will treat them as zero values). In reality, the experience of the modeller will prove invaluable when selecting, understanding and using the required built-in facilities offered by the chosen spreadsheet. Once the modeller has decided that a built-in facility is suitable, an impression can be made about the volume and complexity of the calculations which must be included in the model. Obviously, this will affect the size and structure of the model.

OPTIMAL MEMORY ALLOCATION

Historically, the development of larger and more complex spreadsheet models was influenced by the volume of available computer memory. This limitation often resulted in simplifications to the models developed, and, in turn, diminished the ability of the model to depict reality. The availability of memory was not only influenced by the complexity of the model developed but also by the type of spreadsheet used. Moreover, the structure and layout of the model had to be influenced not only by process complexity but also by consideration of memory. Specifically, three types of memory allocation are used by spreadsheets: sparse matrix, semi-sparse matrix and dense matrix.

Sparse matrix

Generally, spreadsheets using this type of memory allocation were only practical for the development of small models, where the availability of memory is unlikely to be a constraint. If an older PC and spreadsheet is to be utilized by the model user, this method of memory allocation is not efficient because each live cell in the model is allocated memory. AsEasyAs is one spreadsheet which uses sparse matrix memory allocation.

Semi-sparse matrix

The more recent versions of Lotus 1-2-3 use the 'semi-sparse' matrix type of memory allocation. In this spreadsheet, small rectangular blocks of cells are allocated memory, whereas any columns which are completely empty are not allocated memory. Another spreadsheet which utilizes this type of memory allocation is Multiplan. In Multiplan memory is allocated in blocks of rows. As a consequence, memory can be saved using this spreadsheet by inserting blank rows into a model rather than blank columns.

Dense matrix

For a spreadsheet utilizing dense matrix memory allocation, the top left and bottom right live cells of the model are identified and memory is allocated to the rectangle of cells so defined. In utilizing a package which uses this type of memory allocation, it is unwise to leave a large proportion of cells empty within a model. That is, the model should be squeezed as tightly as possible into the top left-hand corner of the spreadsheet. The earliest version of Lotus 1-2-3 used this type of memory allocation.

DEFINING THE LAYOUT OF THE MODEL

Any mathematical model or computer program has three main 'functional' components: input, process and output of data. Specifically, the area of process consists of formulae, calculations and, where appropriate, spreadsheet code which can be activated automatically. To design a user-friendly spreadsheet model, it is good practice to use a structured layout which ensures that these functional areas remain separate and self-contained. Investment of time in the design of the model and its layout will facilitate end-user understanding and simplify any maintenance or amendments to the model which may have to take place. As a business scenario changes, a clear layout of the model representing the problem (i.e. designing the model using separate sections) should permit the necessary modifications to take place.

The block structure

A useful way of designing a formal model is by using a block structure. The most important feature of this design is that the self-contained sections of the model are allocated non-overlapping blocks of cells. All of these self-contained blocks should have dimensions of whole numbers of (spreadsheet) screens. This will facilitate ease of navigation around the model and also ensure that the model retains a block structure, where each section remains separate and self-contained.

The layout of a large spreadsheet model can be presented in one of three ways, where each method is based on a block structure. Specifically, if availability of memory is to prove a limitation, the choice of layout should be influenced by the type of memory allocation utilized by the spreadsheet. Although memory allocation is unlikely to be a problem nowadays, the constraints of the past yielded a number of user-friendly structures which proved useful when developing formal spreadsheet models. Figure 3.4 illustrates the most efficient way of structuring a model which is constrained by semi-sparse matrix allocation, whereas Figure 3.5 illustrates the most appropriate layout where the package adopts the dense matrix method.

In Figures 3.4 and 3.5, each of the self-contained blocks have been assigned a descriptive name. Certain blocks deal with the issue of *user support*, and are particularly important when the model user has limited spreadsheet experience. The blocks which belong to this category include model introduction, on-screen help facilities and the on-screen model map. The remaining blocks are *functional* in nature and deal with issues of data input, process and output, as well as model automation.

Note that in both Figure 3.4 and Figure 3.5, the 'model' section of the layout consists of formulae, calculations and other processing of data.

Alternatively, if the spreadsheet allows a model to be designed using multiple sheets, then a layout similar to that illustrated in Figure 3.6 would be appropriate. Version 5 of Excel permits the use of multiple sheets. In such a layout, each of the self-contained sections of the model can be housed on an individual spreadsheet, which can be subsequently linked. In a multi-sheet model, each separate page can be accessed by clicking on **TAB** keys which are located at the bottom of the worksheet. As a default, these tabs have the labels A, B, C, etc. It is good practice to replace these labels with meaningful (unique) names for each page in the formal model structure, i.e. INTRO, HELP, etc. Once the sheets have been developed, they should be defined

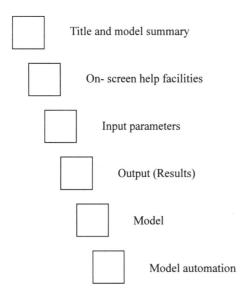

Title and model summary

On- screen help facilities

Input parameters

Output (Results)

Model

Model automation

Figure 3.4 Layout for semi-sparse matrix memory allocation

Title and model summary	Input parameters	Output (Results)
On-screen help facilities	Model	Model automation

Figure 3.5 Layout for dense matrix memory allocation

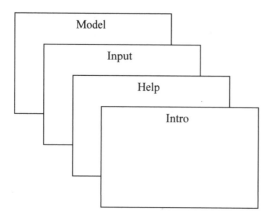

Figure 3.6   Layout for a model designed using multiple sheets

as a GROUP; and by doing so, calculations housed on the model page can reference variables stored on the model's input sheet. This method of model design is particularly useful because each separate section can be stored in the top left-hand corner of the relevant sheet, thus facilitating user navigation.

Because of recent enhancements to the PC, memory allocation should no longer prove a limiting factor to the modeller. Nevertheless, any of the block structures described will still prove useful and should be employed when a formal model needs to be developed. In particular, the modeller may prefer to utilize the layout pictured in Figure 3.4. This is arguably more user-friendly than the layout presented in Figure 3.5 since rows and columns can be added or deleted to an individual block without corrupting any of the code housed in the adjacent blocks of the model. This concept is illustrated in Figure 3.7 where the process section of the model has been increased in size by adding rows and columns. The modifications to the dimensions of this block do not affect the contents of any other block within the model. In contrast, modification to the second structure in Figure 3.7 has resulted in four blocks being affected. Moreover, it should be stressed that the layout illustrated in Figure 3.5 should really only be used for models to be used on older PCs where allocation of memory is likely to be a critical factor.

For any of the structures described, it is good practice for the modeller to allocate *whole numbers of screens* to each of the separate blocks. Such an allocation of space allows the end user to employ the key combinations available on the PC keyboard to quickly access the different parts of the model. The appropriate key combinations which can be utilized within a model written in Excel are shown in Figure 3.8.

THE SIMPLE 'CONTRACTOR'S' MODEL

Now that a formal model structure has been defined, the layout of the 'contractor's' model can be addressed. This model needs to be formal and presented in a user-friendly way for a model user with limited spreadsheet experience. As a consequence, there are two areas which need to be considered:

- User support
- Functional areas of the model

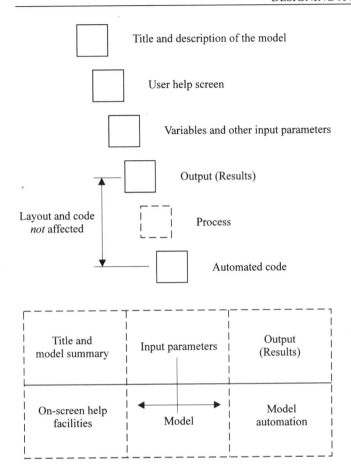

Figure 3.7   How the block layouts facilitate model amendments

Function	Purpose
CTRL + PAGE DOWN	Move right one screen
CTRL + PAGE UP	Move left one screen
PAGE UP	Move up one screen
PAGE DOWN	Move down one screen
CTRL + HOME	Move the cursor to cell A1
F5 cell	Go to a specified cell

Figure 3.8   Common key combinations available on the PC keyboard

In the area of user support, the end user requires a detailed model introduction, help facilities and an on-screen map which may be accessed if the end user wishes to navigate around the model.

The functional areas of the model must include an input screen (where the dimensions of a new building can be entered), a process screen (housing the necessary calculations) and an output block displaying the output variables cost and duration which pertain to the contract

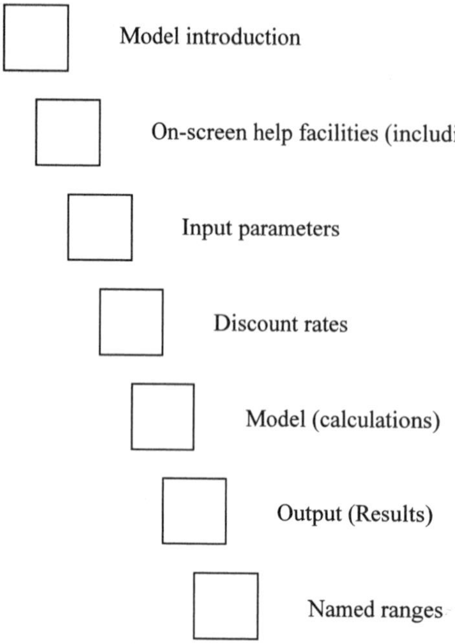

Model introduction

On-screen help facilities (including map)

Input parameters

Discount rates

Model (calculations)

Output (Results)

Named ranges

Figure 3.9   Block structure for the 'contractor's' model

under consideration. Additionally, a separate block will also be required to house information on contract discount rates. The content of each of these blocks will be described in Chapter 4. In building this model, version 4 of Microsoft Excel has been used, and as a consequence the model will use a two-dimensional structure. Figure 3.9 illustrates the block structure that will be used. This is a more suitable structure than that suggested for the 'contractor's' problem in Figure 2.14 because any structural changes to an individual block will result in minimum alteration to the formal model structure (as illustrated by Figure 3.7).

There is one important difference to note between the structure shown in Figure 3.9 and the general block structure described earlier in the chapter. By comparing Figure 3.9 and Figure 3.5 it should be apparent that the section of model named 'Model automation' is not included in the proposed structure for the 'contractor's' model. In Microsoft Excel the automated spreadsheet code (which is known generically as macro code) is developed and stored on its own separate worksheet, which is then referred to by the spreadsheet housing the model. Depending upon the modelling application, the volume of macro code may be large, and, as a result, any model structure housing this code may become large and cumbersome. As a consequence, the location of this code on its own self-contained sheet should be viewed as a welcome modelling enhancement. Developing and using macros in Microsoft Excel will be introduced formally in Chapter 5.

USING EXCEL EFFICIENTLY

The most efficient way to incorporate calculations onto an Excel spreadsheet is using a 'block (or modular) structure' where every formula included on the spreadsheet refers only to cells located above it. In other words, it is good practice to locate the model's input variables and data towards the top of the spreadsheet and the model's calculations and results towards the bottom. Inspection of Figure 3.9 shows that the modeller intends the input screen and discount rates to be located at the top of the structure and the 'model' and results screens to be situated near the bottom.

Although the model to be developed contains only a few calculations, it is still good practice to use this block structure. Once the reader is confident in developing spreadsheet models in a structured manner, the benefits of efficiency will be gained when Excel is used for more complex modelling applications.

CONCLUSIONS

In this chapter, the different ways in which a spreadsheet model can be designed have been described. In deciding on the layout of a formal model, a simple block structure can be utilized. The most important advantage in employing a block structure is that the modeller can ensure that the important functional areas of data input, process and output remain separate and self-contained. Additionally, the blocks can be arranged on the spreadsheet so that any future structural amendments, say to an individual block of the model (specifically changes to the block's dimensions caused by addition or deletion of rows or columns), will not affect the contents of the other blocks. Moreover, the concept of the block structure has been extended to consider the larger modelling applications where a specific block structure must be adopted to ensure there is an optimal allocation of computer memory to the model. In practice, this will only be of importance to those model users who will be utilizing older PCs and spreadsheets.

Moreover, for larger spreadsheet applications it is important to use the spreadsheet efficiently. In Excel this can be achieved by locating all formulae in cells below those to which they refer. In other words, the input and data screens should be situated at the top of the model structure and the calculations and results towards the bottom. This can be achieved very easily within the framework of the block structures described.

REVIEW QUESTIONS

1. Describe *briefly* how programmers employing high-level languages utilize the 'top-down' method to ensure a structured program design.
2. What are the advantages of the 'top-down' method?
3. In the utilization of a spreadsheet model designed without structure, what is the main source of end-user error?
4. List the five areas which must be considered in the design of a structured spreadsheet model.
5. In determining the suitability of a spreadsheet, give examples where:
   (a) A hand calculator
   (b) A high-level programming language
   (c) Customized application software
   would be more appropriate.
6. What are the advantages of employing a spreadsheet when developing a formal business model?
7. In utilizing a built-in function offered by a spreadsheet, what problems might a modeller encounter? Illustrate with examples specific to your spreadsheet.
8. Describe *briefly* the terms:
   (a) Sparse matrix

    (b) Semi-sparse matrix

    (c) Dense matrix

9. Sketch the most appropriate type of structure for a modelling application where memory allocation may prove critical, when the spreadsheet uses:

    (a) Semi-sparse matrix

    (b) Dense matrix

10. If a spreadsheet permits the use of multiple sheets, sketch a suitable block structure.

11. When memory allocation is unlikely to prove critical, sketch the most appropriate block structure and describe its suitability to the design of the model.

12. Why is it useful for each block to have dimensions consisting of whole numbers of spreadsheet screens?

CASE STUDY QUESTIONS

1. For the investor's problem introduced as a case study question in Chapter 2, a formal model structure is required. The end user has limited spreadsheet experience, and, as a result, the following user-support screens should be included:

   – Model introduction

   – On-screen map

   – Help screens

   Additionally, the following functional screens need to be included in the formal model structure:

   – Input

   – Process

   – Results

   – A screen to house a data table

   The role of a data table in a formal model structure is described in Chapters 4 and 8. At this stage, a formal definition will not be introduced. However, it is necessary to incorporate a block into the formal model structure to allow for its inclusion.

   Using these specifications provided by the end user, design a paper-based spreadsheet map, using the structure shown in Figure 3.7.

2. To build an appropriately sized model, the following dimensions for each screen will be appropriate:

Model introduction	1×1
On-screen map	1×1
Help screens	2×1
Input	1×1
Process	2×1
Results	1×1
A screen to house a data table	1×1

where dimensions $a \times b$ mean a screens in height and b screens in width. The process block is larger than the blocks which house the model's input and output so that it can accommodate the necessary on-screen documentation. Model documentation will be addressed in Chapter 7.

3. After the block structure has been developed, add screen titles to each separate block and save the structure as **INVEST.XLS**.

FOUR

DETERMINING THE CONTENTS OF A FORMAL SPREADSHEET MODEL

OVERVIEW

This chapter describes the role and contents of each separate, self-contained section resident in a formal spreadsheet model. The issue of formulae presentation is addressed by considering the functional blocks used in the model. At the end of the chapter, a number of additional concepts are considered, including the use of graphs in a formal model.

OBJECTIVES

After reading this chapter and working through the questions, the reader will be able to:

- Recognize the role and contents of each separate, self-contained section of a spreadsheet model
- Represent the relationships identified in the conceptual model using an appropriate combination of mathematical formulae (constructed by the modeller) and suitable built-in spreadsheet facilities
- Ensure that the formulae used in the model are both readable and understandable for modeller and model user

INTRODUCTION

In this chapter, the role and contents of each of the self-contained blocks included in a formal spreadsheet model are described. To achieve this, reference is made to the simple but formal 'contractor's' model written in Microsoft Excel.

In identifying the contents of a formal model, a user-friendly approach to constructing mathematical formulae within a spreadsheet model is described. At the end of the chapter, there is general discussion on the inclusion of graphs within a formal model. It is assumed that the reader will be familiar with the 'mechanics' of constructing a graph, and as a consequence the issues raised are not spreadsheet-specific.

DETERMINING THE CONTENTS OF EACH SELF-CONTAINED BLOCK

At the end of the previous chapter, a block structure was defined for the 'contractor's' model and was pictured in Figure 3.9. The self-contained blocks included in the agreed structure fall into two categories:

- User support facilities
- Functional sections of the model

The user support facilities should always be included in a formal model and their role is to assist the end user in using the model as effectively as possible by providing a user-friendly modelling environment. These screens include:

- A model introduction
- On-screen help facilities
- An on-screen map

The content and size of these blocks will vary from model to model. Moreover, the volume and size of the help facilities will also be dependent upon on the skills and spreadsheet experience of the end user.

As a minimum, the functional areas of the model will consist of:

- Input
- Process (calculations)
- Output (Results)

Again, these blocks will vary in size and their contents in volume and complexity for different modelling applications. In practice, the size of these functional blocks will be much more variable than the user-support facilities listed above.

Finally, a number of spreadsheet models may incorporate additional modelling facilities including *lookup tables* and *data tables*. The inclusion of these facilities will depend upon the modelling situation and their usefulness should be determined by the modeller prior to any spreadsheet development. The 'contractor's' model incorporates a lookup table to store the different hourly rates charged for a contract, but not a data table. However, both facilities are described in this chapter for completeness.

In this section of the chapter, the role and contents of each block are described in detail. To do this, reference is made to the simple, but structured, 'contractor's' model. Each individual self-contained block in this block will be considered and each area of the model is illustrated by a screen output.

There is one major advantage in using this model to illustrate the concept of structured spreadsheet modelling. The calculations and modelling processes are easy to understand and the volume of computation is small. While the model is developed using Microsoft Excel, the code developed and the concepts are described in a general manner and, as a result, are readily transferable to other spreadsheets. Although the 'contractor's' problem is simple, the formal structure developed includes most of the features usually found in a formal model, i.e. formulae constructed by the modeller, utilization of built-in functions and an appropriate degree of model automation (this will be introduced in the next chapter). Moreover, the model is based on a formal block structure and incorporates most of the features described in the introduction to this chapter.

USER-SUPPORT FACILITIES

Introduction

The introductory screen(s) of a model are arguably the most important area of the program from the point of view of an end user with limited experience of spreadsheets. As a minimum, this block should contain a model title, a reference to the modelling personnel and a

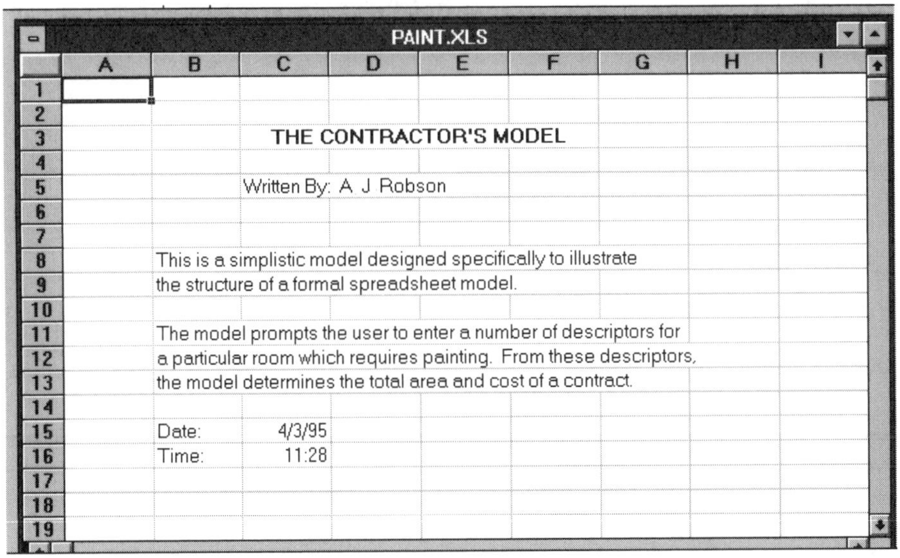

Figure 4.1   The introduction screen found in the 'contractor's' model

non-technical description of the model. Figure 4.1 shows the introduction screen used in the 'contractor's' model. From an end user's perspective, the introduction represents the most important part of the model's internal documentation. As a consequence, the modeller should ensure that this screen is the first accessed by the end user on retrieval of the model. In the 'contractor's' model, the introduction screen is simple and consists of a title, reference to the modeller and a description of the model's role in the decision-making process.

Since the introduction block is usually small and its content is similar for most modelling applications (i.e. model title and summary), it is best located in the top left-hand corner of the model skeleton. Moreover, a suitable location for any on-screen help facilities would be adjacent to the introduction block. The on-screen help facilities constructed for the 'contractor's' model are described below.

Help facilities

Again, for an end user with limited knowledge of spreadsheets, the on-screen or worksheet help facilities play an important role in supporting the effective use of a structured model. In practice, such facilities should incorporate instructions on how to use the model most effectively. For example, if the model contains a pop-up user menu, instructions on how to activate the different menu options should form part of this on-screen help facility. However, it may be more appropriate to decentralize any detailed description of the actual model processes to the relevant model screens and provide a non-technical description of their purpose in the model's user guide. The detailed spreadsheet description and the user guide form part of the model's documentation and are described in Chapter 7. The help facilities pictured in Figure 4.2 have been included in the 'contractor's' model and deal solely with utilization of the model's menu facility.

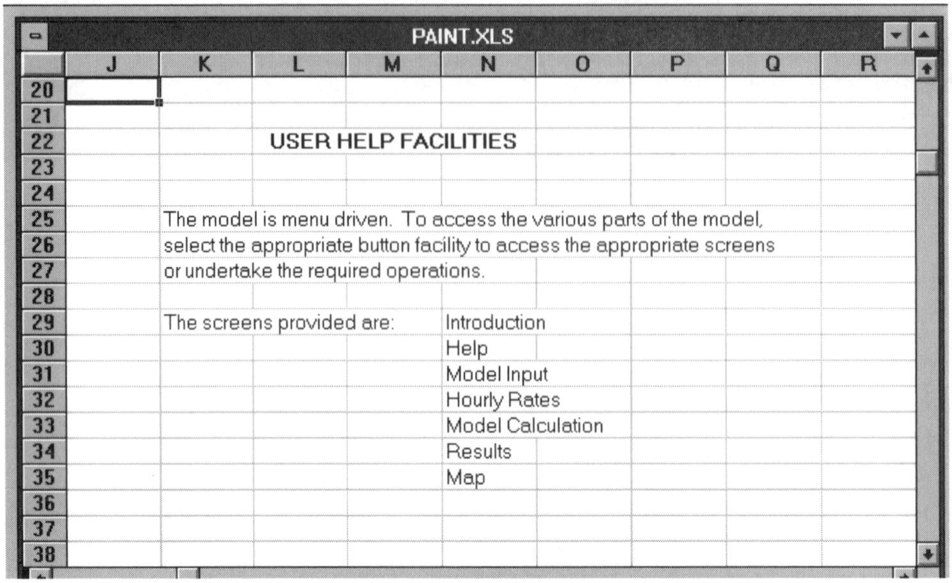

Figure 4.2 The help screen incorporated in the 'contractor's' model

On-screen mapping details

An additional help facility which may be incorporated into a model is a block showing a map of the spreadsheet model. This map may be a diagrammatical representation of the model, a set of cell references, or a combination of diagram and cell references. Depending upon the size of the model developed, this map may be located within the help block, as in Figure 4.3, or within its own self-contained screen(s), as pictured in Figure 4.4.

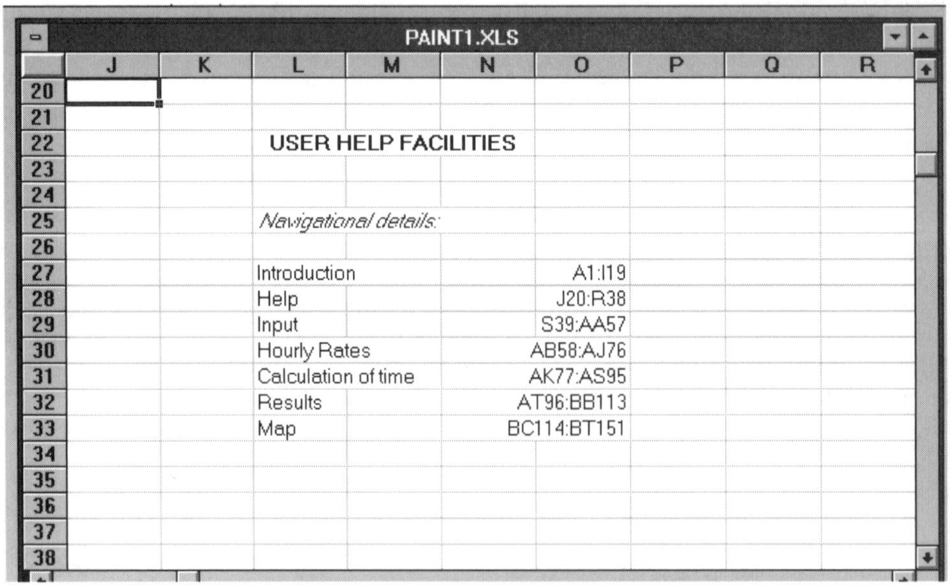

Figure 4.3 Top-level navigational details used in the 'contractor's' model

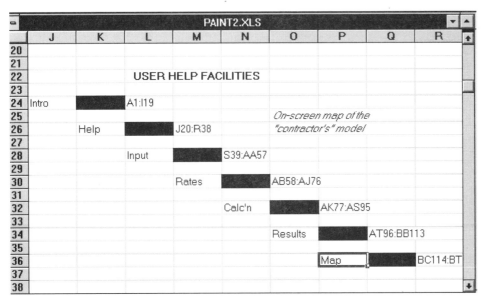

Figure 4.4   On-screen mapping details for the 'contractor's' model

For small modelling applications, it may be suitable to incorporate 'top-level' mapping details within the main help screen. Figure 4.3 illustrates how this could have been achieved for the 'contractor's' model. The mapping details included in Figure 4.3 provide the cell references of each separate block in the model. Such information is useful, because the model user can then utilize the appropriate key combinations described in the last chapter (i.e. the **F5** key which activates the Goto prompt, followed by the appropriate cell reference or cell name) to access the required part of the model.

In contrast, Figure 4.4 gives a pictorial representation of the model, providing a diagrammatical overview of the block structure used, combined with the cell reference of each self-contained block.

FUNCTIONAL SECTIONS OF THE MODEL

Input

The variables located on the input screen(s) should be those whose values are likely to alter for each application of the model. Other parameters used in the model whose values are non-variable can be hard-coded, i.e. their values can be coded into the appropriate formulae. Examples of non-variable model parameters in the contractor's model include the size of doors and windows, which have been assumed as standard. In this model, the variables which alter for each different contract are:

- Length of the building
- Height of the building
- Width of the building
- Number of doors
- Number of windows

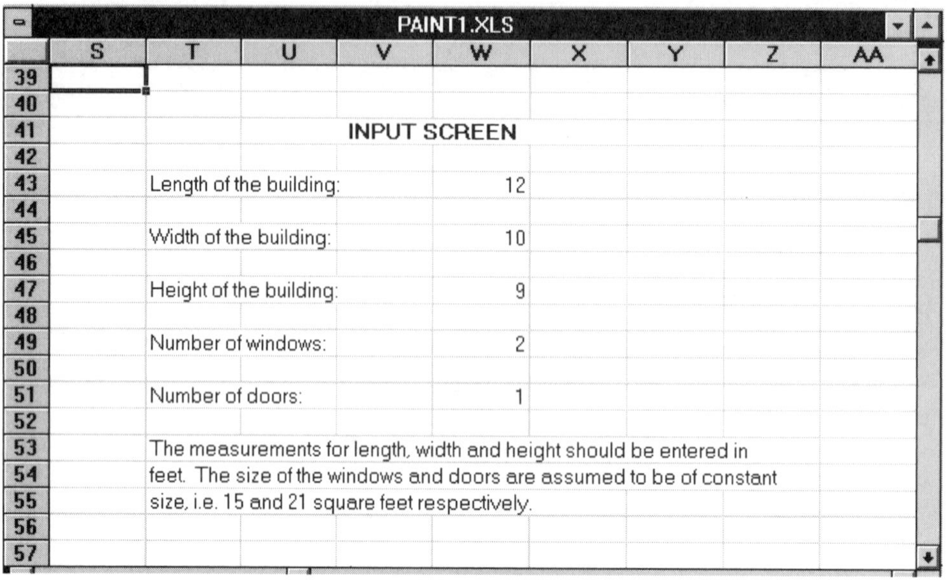

Figure 4.5 Model input screen containing input variables only

These represent the input variables of the model, which is consistent with the conceptual model described in Chapter 2. Figure 4.5 shows an appropriate input screen. This screen deals *only* with the input and storage of these variables. In addition, the screen provides the end user with details on the appropriate units of measurement, i.e. the length, width and height of the building are to be measured in feet.

Perhaps the most important feature of this input screen is that *no formulae or model processes* are present. The model has been well structured since all of the input variables are located 'outside' the process section of the model. Moreover, the formulae housed on the process screens will *reference* the cells containing the model's input variables. Constructing the formulae in this way permits the model user to change the values of these parameters without having to edit any of the model's formulae. As a consequence, this allows the model user to easily enter the dimensions of a new building and calculate the time and cost for the corresponding contract. In more complex models, the end user can experiment by considering a range of scenarios. By providing a structure where the input parameters are located 'outside' the model's calculations, this process is greatly simplified. End-user experimentation is described in Chapter 8.

Moreover, by utilizing a block structure like that shown in Figure 3.9 in the previous chapter, the modeller can reduce the possibility that an end user with little knowledge of spreadsheets will input the model's parameters in the wrong cells and, in doing so, corrupt the model's code. Additionally, the modeller may need to ensure that only reasonable values can be input for these parameters, e.g. the number of doors is entered as a number which is an integer and is greater than zero. This can be achieved by automating the input routine. An appropriate procedure will be described in Chapters 5 and 6.

To ensure that the formulae developed to reference these input variables are as understandable as possible, it is good practice to utilize cell and range names in the creation of any mathematical formulae. Most spreadsheets permit the modeller to name individual cells or blocks of cells and, in Excel, the naming of cells can be achieved by highlighting the individual cell or block of cells and invoking the command:

Fo**r**mula
Define Name

If a formula which references *named* cells is moved because of structural amendments to the model, the use of range names can help minimize any corruption of the affected code. Moreover, each of the self-contained blocks can also be named. For the screen shown in Figure 4.5, the input variables have been named LENGTH, WIDTH, HEIGHT, DOORS and WINDOWS and the input screen has been named input_screen. If the cells in a model containing either variables or data are named, the presentation and understanding of its formulae are enhanced, aiding both modeller and model user. This is demonstrated later in the chapter, again with reference to the 'contractor's' model.

Model

The model screens should represent the internal processes and calculations undertaken in the program. That is, this block should contain the mathematical relationships which represent the business problem and have been identified during the development of the conceptual model. As described earlier in this chapter, these mathematical relationships consist of formulae and calculations which may be constructed by the modeller or involve part or full utilization of the appropriate built-in facilities offered by the spreadsheet. In the 'contractor's' model, the conceptual model highlighted a number of factors which influence the duration of a decorating contract. These factors will be represented by the formulae resident on the model and results screens. In general, the complexity of the spreadsheet code will be influenced by the complexity of the conceptual model and the power and flexibility of the spreadsheet. In general, there must be consideration of:

- The skills of the modeller *and* the model user. Specifically, a complex model may be mis-trusted by those responsible for making decisions and, as a consequence, the output it yields may be difficult to implement.
- The capabilities of the spreadsheet. For example, if the modeller wishes to develop a causal model (as included in the 'contractor's' model), the capabilities of any built-in regression facility offered by the spreadsheet should be addressed. In particular, certain spreadsheets permit the use of only one independent variable.
- The availability of data to support the model's application.
- The time and cost of developing the model and its subsequent benefit to the end user.

In the simple 'contractor's' model, it can be seen from the conceptual model that the only variable which has a measurable effect on a contract's duration is the size or area of the building. Moreover, this variable is also easy to calculate.

In determining the relationship that exists between duration and area, the modeller must construct the appropriate mathematical relationship. As described in Chapter 2, this can be achieved either by using the built-in Regression facility housed in Excel's Analysis Toolkit or alternatively by using the **SLOPE( )** and **INTERCEPT( )** commands offered by the spreadsheet. Figure 4.6 illustrates the model screen incorporating the regression output within the 'contractor's' model. In evaluating this relationship, the modeller must ensure that a *representative sample of data* has been collected. The data which has been entered into cells AL82:AL91 (named SAMPLE by highlighting the block of cells and activating **Fo**r**mula **D**efine Name**) represents this sample.

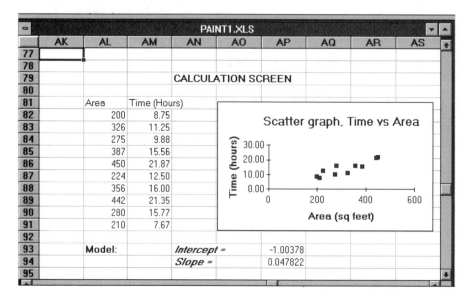

Figure 4.6 Model screen displaying regression analysis

Additionally, the modeller must ensure that the regression equation developed is valid. There are a number of established tests which may be undertaken and these can be performed using the powerful features of the spreadsheet. These tests are described in a number of well established statistical tests, and, in order to concentrate on the modelling concepts, they will not be considered in this chapter. Assuming the relationship determined is valid, the regression output generated can then be used in the formal model. Any additional analysis, i.e. the graphs and calculations produced to support the tests of validity, should not be incorporated into the formal model (i.e. the 'contractor's' model) but saved as a separate spreadsheet. In turn, the spreadsheet containing the test results should be referenced in the (main) model's external documentation (see Chapter 7).

Further testing of the relationship identified in the conceptual model and the regression output incorporated in the spreadsheet program may be required. In particular, the end user may require the model to perform to a predetermined level of accuracy. In short, these considerations may be iterative in nature and will require investment of both modeller time and expertise. Specifically, if the relationship between time and area is found to be invalid, the modeller will have to consider additional independent variables which may have been identified during the development of the conceptual model.

The simple regression equation which quantifies the relationship between time and area is:

$$\text{TIME} = -1.004 + 0.048 \times \text{AREA}$$

For a given contract, time will be estimated using this relationship after an appropriate formula has been constructed. As a consequence, the cells containing the coefficients −1.004 and 0.048 have been named INTER and SLOPE respectively.

Additionally, a number of other formulae are housed in the model. These include the calculation of contract time and cost. Since both of these variables represent the model's output, they have been located on the model's output screen.

A useful way of constructing formulae in Excel is by using the Paste Function facility. This may be activated by selecting:

Fo_r_mula Pas_t_e Function

which results in the chosen function being pasted into the resident cell on the spreadsheet. The modeller simply has to define the relevant parameters inside the selected function once this has been done. For example, using **NPV( )**, the modeller would have to define the reference to the discount rate and range of cashflows. The advantage of using the Paste Function facility is that it ensures that the modeller enters the function correctly into the model and especially in the definition of each required parameter.

Output (Results)

In practice, the output or results block will be of most interest to the end user because it contains the information which may be used in the decision-making process. As a consequence, clarity and presentation are of utmost importance. To enhance model presentation, a number of spreadsheets incorporate facilities which can be used to customize the appearance of these screens so that they resemble (as near as possible) the general report format of the organization. These facilities are described in Chapter 9. If the model is to be used frequently, then the end user may wish the results screen to incorporate details of time and date. Many spreadsheets offer built-in facilities which can be formatted to display the time and date of model use in an appropriate way. For example, Excel offers the function **NOW( )** which may be formatted to show the date and time of model use using **Format Date** and **Format Time** respectively.

In addition, the output screens must include all of the information required by the end user. Consequently, both the modeller and model user should be in agreement on these details. Figure 4.7 shows the output screen from the 'contractor's' model. The main details included on this screen are:

- The dimensions of the building
- The number of doors and windows
- The calculation of contract size (i.e. area of building)
- The estimates of contract duration and cost

At the top of this results screen, there is a box which houses the building's dimensions, underneath which the numbers of doors and windows are located. These five values represent the parameters of the model, i.e. their values determine the size of a building and, in turn, the duration and cost of a particular contract. For a given contract, the value of each of these parameters will be input into the model as illustrated in Figure 4.5. Moreover, their inclusion on the results screen should involve *cell referencing* the input block. In this model, each parameter has been named as described, and therefore the results screen references five named cells: LENGTH, WIDTH, HEIGHT, WINDOWS and DOORS.

In addition, this screen houses four formulae which have been written by the modeller and are described below. These formulae undertake the following operations:

1. Determining the size (area) of the building (stored in cell AX110)
2. Estimating the duration of the contract using the regression equation (cell AX111)

	AT	AU	AV	AW	AX	AY	AZ	BA	BB
96									
97									
98				RESULTS SCREEN					
99									
100			Date:		26/08/94				
101			Time:		14:27				
102									
103			Building dimensions:						
104									
105			Height	Width	Length				
106			9	10	12				
107			Number of doors:		1				
108			Number of Windows:		2				
109									
110			Area to be painted:		345.00				
111			Time taken:		17.50				
112					INTERPOLATION				
113			Cost:		£201.28				
114									

Figure 4.7 The output screen from the 'contractor's' model

3. Determining whether *interpolation* or *extrapolation* has taken place during the prediction of time for a particular contract (cell AX112)
4. Calculating the cost of the contract (cell AX113)

1. *Determining the size (area) of the building*
   The input parameters of the contractor's model are length, width and height of the building plus the number of doors and windows. Using these parameters, the area of the building can be determined using the formula:

$$= 2*HEIGHT*(LENGTH + WIDTH) - ((DOORS*21) + (WINDOWS*15))$$

The formula has assumed that doors and windows are of a standard size, i.e. 21 and 15 square feet respectively. The cell containing this formula has been named AREA.

It should be apparent that, by using cell names, the formula presented above is easy to read and understand. If cell references were used instead, the formula would resemble:

$$= 2*W47*(W43 + W45)-((W51*21) + (W49*15))$$

which is obviously less understandable. Naming cells will help both the modeller (who may be responsible for the model's maintenance) and the end user (who will use the model regularly).

2. *Estimating the duration of the contract*
   The estimated duration of a particular contract is provided by the formula:

$$= INTER + (SLOPE*AREA)$$

The cells named by the modeller as INTER and SLOPE have been provided as the part of the regression output housed on the process screen of the model and were described earlier in the chapter. The cell containing duration has been named TIME.

3. *Interpolation or extrapolation*
   The formula in cell AX112 indicates to the model user whether the forecast made by the model involves INTERPOLATION (prediction for a building whose size is within the range

of areas used to quantify the relationship between time and area) or EXTRAPOLATION (prediction outside the range). The mathematical statement written in this cell utilizes the built-in **IF( )**, **MAX( )** and **MIN( )** functions (which have equivalent functions in a most spreadsheets) and the logical **OR** facility offered by Microsoft Excel. The name SAMPLE refers to the range of cells AL82:AL91 on the model screen. The formula used is:

= IF(OR(AREA < MIN(SAMPLE),AREA > MAX(SAMPLE)),"EXTRAP","INTER")

In the contract illustrated in Figure 4.7, the building under consideration has an area of 345 square feet. The range of areas considered in the evaluation of the regression equation is 200 to 450 square feet, so the corresponding message is INTERPOLATION. In providing output of such a statistical nature, the model's user guide must provide an adequate explanation for a non-technical end user. Documentation of formulae and the development of a model user-guide are addressed in Chapter 7, again with reference to the 'contractor's' model.

4. *Calculating contract cost*

Finally, the cost of the contract can be calculated by utilizing the relevant information stored in a table of data called RATES. The cost is calculated by using the built-in **VLOOKUP()** function (described later in this chapter). The appropriate formula is:

= TIME∗VLOOKUP(TIME,$RATES,1)

This cell has been called COST.

As illustrated, all four formulae described above incorporate named individual cells or ranges of cells. This makes the formulae much easier to understand and assists both modeller and end user in relating the formulae both to the conceptual model (described in Chapter 2) *and* to reality.

In general, as a modelling situation becomes more complex, the corresponding mathematical relationships and spreadsheet formulae may increase in complexity. As a formula increases in complexity, the time taken to write, test and debug the resultant code will also increase. These processes can be simplified by using range names as described and also by *separating the complex formulae into small, separate but related parts*. For example, the most complex formula used in the 'contractor's' model is the one which indicates whether interpolation or extrapolation has taken place when the duration of a contract has been estimated. This formula could be split into three shorter, related parts, i.e:

= IF(AREA < MIN(SAMPLE),1,0) name LESS
= IF(AREA > MIN(SAMPLE),1,0) name MORE
= IF(OR(LESS = 1,MORE = 1),"EXTRAP","INTER")

By doing this the spreadsheet code becomes easier to follow.

Additional model processes

Depending upon the complexity of the modelling situation and the skills and requirement of the end user, some or all of the model's operations may be *automated*. A model's operation may be automated by writing a piece of spreadsheet code called a *macro*. A macro is a set of (related) instructions which can be activated automatically by a single keystroke or by selecting an option from a pop-up user menu. In developing a suite of macros, the modeller and model user should be aware of the trade-off between automation and model informality. Macros and model automation will be introduced formally, with reference to the 'contractor's' model, in Chapter 5.

As indicated in Chapter 3, any macro code developed in Excel is housed on its own self-contained worksheet which can then be accessed by the model. Since this section of code is arguably the most variable in size, it is particularly useful to have the macro code stored 'adjacent to' rather than 'part of' the main model structure.

For an end user with limited spreadsheet or programming knowledge, it is likely that the code housed in this block is meaningless, and by housing it on its own worksheet, it is also likely that such an end user will perhaps never view the contents of this sheet. Nevertheless, structure and presentation of this code is still important, and will be addressed in the next chapter. This presentation is aimed primarily at those modelling personnel who will be responsible for maintaining and updating the model.

In general, the role of the macros must be clear to the modeller before coding begins, *and most importantly the amount of automation should be dictated by the needs of the model's end user*.

This book assumes that the end user of the 'contractor's' model has limited knowledge of spreadsheet operations. As a consequence, certain operations need to be automated:

- Input and testing of the model's parameters (i.e. the dimensions of the building to be painted) by providing a user-friendly interface between the spreadsheet and the end user
- Print-out of the model's output
- Saving the updated model
- Exiting from Excel
- Efficient navigation around the formal model structure

Once these features have been discussed and agreed by the two parties, coding can begin. However, as a *minimum*, it is good practice to incorporate a degree of automation into most formal models, if only to facilitate efficient user navigation around the formal model structure.

Hourly rates (lookup table)

In the 'contractor's' model the hourly rate for an individual contract will vary according to contract size. The most efficient way of using this 'semi-variable' information in a formal model is by listing all of the possible rates and corresponding contract times into a 'lookup table'. A lookup table is simply a table of data stored in the spreadsheet model. The process of searching this table for relevant information is usually described as 'lookup' (i.e. looking up the relevant information). In practice, this type of table will contain data which is used frequently within the model but whose values do not change regularly. As a consequence, the values can be stored within the model as a separate stand-alone table. In the 'contractor's' model, the hourly rate for undertaking a contract is variable because the company operates a discount scheme for contracts of larger duration. As a consequence, this data forms a table of hourly rates rather than a single rate. Figure 4.8 illustrates the appropriate lookup table. The table consists of two columns, the first containing the duration of the contact and the second the rate per hour. Additionally, the on-screen documentation provides details on how the information is used.

It is important to note that, in the creation of the lookup table within a model developed using Excel, the modeller should ensure that both columns of data are *adjacent*.

	AB	AC	AD	AE	AF	AG	AH	AI	AJ
58									
59									
60			HOURLY RATES FOR THE CONTRACT						
61									
62									
63			Time	Rate		The lookup table is called RATES.			
64						Excel looks up the time in column 1 and			
65			0	£12.75		reads the appropriate hourly rate from			
66			10	£11.50		column 2. This is achieved by using the			
67			20	£10.85		VLOOKUP() command			
68			30	£9.75					
69			40	£9.50					
70			50	£9.00					
71			100	£8.00					
72									
73									
74									
75									
76									

Figure 4.8 Lookup table used in the 'contractor's' model

Since this information will be used in one of the model's calculations, it should be named. In the simple model, the table has been named RATES. In order to call up the appropriate hourly rate for a given contract, the modeller needs to type:

$$= VLOOKUP(TIME,\$RATES,1)$$

The variable TIME corresponds to the prediction of contract duration made using the regression equation housed on the model block and the size of contract stored on the results screen. The number '1' tells the spreadsheet to compare TIME with those durations stored in column 1 of the lookup table. Finally, to determine the costs of the contract the modeller will multiply the selected hourly rate by the estimated duration, namely TIME. This is achieved by using the formula:

$$= TIME*VLOOKUP(TIME,\$RATES,1)$$

This formula is stored in cell AX113 and was described earlier in the chapter.

Referring to the table of contract rates, the first rate is £12.75 per hour, and is charged for contracts of zero up to but not including 10 hours duration (0 and 10 being the first two values of time stored in the table). If a given contract is of 15.5 hours duration, the spreadsheet will scan column 1 of the lookup table. The value 15.5 is less than 20 stored in the table (cell AD67) and so Excel will use the hourly rate corresponding to the previous duration, i.e. 10.0 hours, whose hourly rate is stored in cell AE66.

If a 'lookup' facility did not exist within the spreadsheet, it would be necessary to construct a relatively complex formula to compute the hourly rate. The formula would look like:

$$=IF(TIME>=100,8,IF(AND(TIME>=50,TIME<100),9,IF( )))$$

Obviously such a formula is much more difficult to construct, understand and, whenever appropriate, much more difficult to amend. Finally, it may also be useful to provide on-screen documentation to support the use of a lookup table in a formal model. In the simple model described, this documentation should indicate who is responsible for setting the hourly rates for the contracts undertaken and the date of the previous amendment.

Data tables

The final type of 'functional' block which may used by the modeller is not included in the 'contractor's' model, but for a number of modelling applications serves a very useful purpose. This facility is called the *data table*. A data table is a built-in spreadsheet facility which provides a record of the consequence of changing the values of one or two of the model's input variables. This record can help the end user identify the optimal or 'best' solution to a modelling situation and it also demonstrates how variable the model solution is to changes in the values of the selected parameters. In particular, the data table can be used to facilitate end-user experimentation. Being consistent with the block structure described in the last two chapters, the record created by the data table facility should be housed within its own self-contained block, preferably adjacent to the model's output. The application of data tables to model experimentation is described fully in Chapter 8 with reference to a specific formal model. A data table has not been incorporated into the contractor's model, since its inclusion is not appropriate.

GRAPHICAL DISPLAY OF DATA WITHIN A FORMAL SPREADSHEET MODEL

In developing a formal spreadsheet model, the modeller may consider it appropriate to present some of the model's output as a graph. Many of the modern spreadsheets incorporate a graphics facility and it is assumed that the reader is able to construct a graph using a spreadsheet. This process is particularly easy using Excel because of the user-friendly ChartWizard facility provided by the spreadsheet. This facility was demonstrated diagrammatically in Chapter 2. In this part of the book, the 'mechanics' of constructing graphs using a spreadsheet will not be described, but instead a set of guidelines will be provided which will ensure that graphs are properly used within a formal model structure.

Selecting the appropriate graph

Before constructing a graph using the spreadsheet, the modeller should be aware of the nature of the data to be presented and must ensure that an *appropriate* graph is selected. In short, there are likely to be two main types of data which will be encountered by the modeller: nominal data and quantitative data.

Nominal data   Nominal data is that data which may be divided into non-numerical categories. In other words, names are used to describe the different categories instead of numbers or numeric intervals. Example of nominal data include nationality, car manufacturers, destination of holiday-makers.

Quantitative data   In contrast, quantitative data is that information which can be measured or quantified. Moreover, such data can be divided into variable ranges which can be classed by size. Quantitative data can be one of two types: continuous or discrete.

Continuous data   This type of data permits a variable to take any value within a continuous range. Examples of continuous quantitative data include salaries, heights and the areas of buildings considered in the 'contractor's' model.

Discrete data   A discrete data set contains data for which only certain values in a predefined interval are permitted. Common examples include the number of patients attending a GP's surgery on a given day (integer values only) and UK shoe sizes (5, $5\frac{1}{2}$, 6, $6\frac{1}{2}$, etc.).

Obviously, the different types of data which can be used within a spreadsheet model should be presented by the appropriate type of graph. Specifically, the *nominal data* should be presented by either a either a *bar chart* or a *pie chart*. In contrast, the *continuous data* should be represented by a *histogram* or *line graph*. In handling continuous data, the modeller should be aware that the histogram is different from the bar chart. Specifically, the bars in the histogram are continuous and non-overlapping whereas those in the bar chart are separate. In practice, most spreadsheets offer bar charts but not histograms. Finally, the *discrete data* described above should be presented using the *bar chart*.

Essential features of the graph

If a graph is to be used as part of the output of a formal spreadsheet model, then it should *as a minimum* contain the following features:

- A main title, usually located at the top of the graph
- Title on the x and y axes
- An appropriate scale on each axis

Additionally, it may be useful to label each of the bars or lines on the graph. This can be achieved by using either the labels or legend facilities offered in most spreadsheet-based graphics facilities. The 'contractor's' model houses a graph depicting the relationship between area of building and duration of contract. This graph is located on the 'model' screen and is shown in Figure 4.6. Here, an appropriate type of graph, the scatter diagram, has been selected by the modeller and all of the features listed above have been incorporated.

If the wrong type of graph is selected or a number of the features listed above are missing, then the resultant graph may be at best difficult to understand or, at worst, misleading or meaningless.

ADDITIONAL CONCEPTS

Once the spreadsheet model has been developed, a final spreadsheet map should be produced. In short, this map will be an updated version of the prototype paper-based map developed prior to spreadsheet construction. In turn, the updated map can form part of the model's external (or technical) documentation. Additionally, the spreadsheet itself should be appropriately documented. To facilitate the development of this internal documentation, the modeller may find it useful to leave the first column of each screen empty to permit the insertion of word-processed documentation. Many spreadsheets incorporate a word-processing facility which may be used in the development of the model's internal (spreadsheet) documentation. The issue of model documentation is described fully in Chapter 7.

Moreover, if any modifications are to be made to the model, then the map should be amended initially, before the actual model is changed in response. On completion of the modelling process, the final model should resemble the documented map. Any remaining blocks of cells, in particular cells used in the processes of model development and testing, should be discarded or stored as alternative spreadsheet files. In particular, these blocks of additional cells may include blank ranges, caused by the relocation of blocks within the formal model structure. Again, these should be deleted.

Moreover, it is easy to produce a map of cell references using Excel. By activating:

Formula

Paste Name followed by **Past List**

the modeller can produce an alphabetic list of all named cells and ranges of cells used in the model. It is good practice to do this for any large, formal model and perhaps the most appropriate place to locate this information on-screen is towards the bottom of the spreadsheet. Moreover, this information will prove useful during the documentation of the model. Figure 4.9 shows the list of named ranges used in the decorator's model. Here individual cells such as input variable LENGTH and output variable AREA have been named as well as each separate screen used in the model. For example, the introductory screen has been named intro_screen.

Once the model is complete, the modeller may wish to enhance its appearance before despatch to the end user. These enhancements may include customizing the appearance of the spreadsheet and protecting certain sections of the model. There are a number of facilities offered by Excel which can be used to enhance model presentation and robustness and are described with reference to the 'contractor's' model in Chapter 9.

Finally, the concept of model efficiency was introduced in Chapter 3. A block structure should be used when building a formal spreadsheet model, and the self-contained sections of the model containing data should be located towards the top of the spreadsheet, while the sections housing calculations should be situated at the bottom. Inspection of the separate parts of the 'contractor's' model show that this efficient structure has been adopted. Moreover, each screen used in this model has been appropriately titled, and, where necessary, on-screen instructions and comments have been included.

	BC	BD	BE	BF	BG	BH	BI	BJ	BK
114									
115									
116									
117				DETAILED SPREADSHEET MAP					
118									
119			doors	=$W$51					
120			extrap	=$AX$112					
121			height	=$W$47					
122			help_screen	=$J$20:$R$38					
123			input_screen	=$S$39:$AA$57					
124			inter	=$AP$93					
125			intro_screen	=$A$1:$I$19					
126			length	=$W$43					
127			model_screen	=$AK$77:$AS$95					
128			Print_Area	=$AT$96:$BB$113					
129			rate_table	=$AD$65:$AE$71					
130			rates_screen	=$AB$58:$AJ$76					
131			ref_screen	=$BC$114:$BK$132					
132			res_screen	=$AT$96:$BB$113					

Figure 4.9 List of named cells and ranges in the model

CONCLUSIONS

In this chapter, the contents of a simple but formal spreadsheet model have been described. A simple application has been used so that the reader can focus on the modelling concepts being introduced.

In particular, two main concepts have been addressed:

- Determining the role and contents of each block of the model
- Construction of the necessary formulae and use of appropriate built-in functions

In determining the layout of a formal model, a simple block structure can be utilized. The most important advantage in employing a block structure is that the modeller can ensure that the functional areas of data input, process and output remain separate and self-contained. Additionally, the blocks can be arranged on the spreadsheet so that any future structural amendments, say to an individual block of the model (specifically changes to the block's dimensions caused by addition or deletion of rows or columns), will not affect the contents of the other blocks.

The role and contents of each separate and self-contained area of a specific formal model (the 'contractor's' model) have been defined. The description is general in nature and is readily transferable to other spreadsheets and modelling applications. In particular, those blocks which are likely to be common to most modelling applications have been indicated.

The construction of formulae and the use of appropriate built-in spreadsheet functions has been addressed by considering the process and output sections housed in the 'contractor's' model. In addressing the presentation of formulae, this chapter has demonstrated how, in Microsoft Excel, individual cells or blocks of cells can be named. Moreover, it has been suggested that all cells used in formulae should be named and that complicated formulae should be separated into smaller, related parts to facilitate end-user understanding. As well as using the name facility for each of the input, process and output variables, it is also useful to name each self-contained block. This ensures that any code referring to a particular block will not be corrupted if structural changes are made to that part of the model.

REVIEW QUESTIONS

1. List the blocks which should be common to most formal spreadsheet models.
2. Considering the list developed in Question 1, which blocks are:
   (a) the most variable in size and content, and
   (b) similar in most modelling applications?
3. Describe the self-contained blocks whose inclusion in formal models is application-dependent.
4. Briefly describe the role and content of each of the following blocks:
   (a) Introduction
   (b) Help facilities
   (c) On-screen spreadsheet map
   (d) Input
   (e) Process (i.e. the 'model')
   (f) Output (Results)
   (g) Lookup tables
   (h) Data tables

5. In the construction of a formula on the spreadsheet, which factors must be considered?
6. What is the advantage in naming individual cells or ranges of cells when constructing formulae?
7. What is the advantage in naming each self-contained block?
8. The two formulae below perform the same function.
   (a) = AX111*VLOOKUP(AX111,AD65:AE71,1)
   (b) = TIME*VLOOKUP(TIME,$RATES,1)
   Which is the more appropriate display? Give reasons for your answer.
9. Describe *briefly* the role of mapping in the development of a structured model.
10. What role does the map take in the future amendments to the model?

CASE STUDY QUESTIONS

In the following questions the contents of each separate block will be identified and the spreadsheet model will be built accordingly.

1. The input screen should house the following parameters:
   - Unit sales in the first year
   - Growth rate per annum (%)
   - Interest rate (%)
   - Cost per unit (£)
   - Price per unit (£)
   - Amount invested (£)
   The input screen should be appropriately labelled.
2. The process screen needs to include the following calculations:
   - Unit sales for years 1 to 5
   - Total cost
   - Total revenue
   - Net cash flow
   - Net present value (NPV) for the investment
3. It may be possible to calculate the NPV using a built-in function provided by the spreadsheet. Refer to a user manual and on-line help facilities to determine if this facility exists. Also check what assumptions are made when using this facility.
4. The output screen should consist of:
   - Unit sales in the first year
   - Growth rate per annum (%)
   - Price per unit (£)
   - Cost per unit (£)
   - Interest rate (%)
   - Amount invested (£)
   - Net present value (NPV) with an indication whether this investment is profitable or unprofitable
   - Date and time details
5. Name each block and each of the input, process and output variables used in the model.
6. The model's introduction screen should contain a meaningful title, a description of the role of the model and details about the model's author.

7. The on-screen map should be a diagrammatical representation of the model, supplemented by cell references for each separate screen.
8. The help screens should contain information regarding how to use the output from the model in the decision-making process. These help facilities will be amended after completing the later chapters of this book.

FIVE

MODEL AUTOMATION (AN INTRODUCTION TO MACROS)

OVERVIEW

This chapter describes the issues which influence the degree of automation to be incorporated into a structured spreadsheet model. The advantages and disadvantages of model automation will be addressed and the term 'macro' will be defined. In turn, three categories of macro will be considered and the importance of both macro documentation and presentation illustrated. At the end of the chapter, a macro facility called the dialog box will be introduced and it will be shown how this facility can be used to provide an interface between a formal model and its end user. Again reference is made to the simple model developed using Microsoft Excel.

OBJECTIVES

After reading this chapter and working through the questions, the reader will be able to:

- Understand the advantages and disadvantages of model automation.
- Define the term 'macro'.
- Define and recognize the role of the different categories of command macro.
- Understand the necessity for macro documentation and presentation.
- Be able to assign buttons to macros to ensure ease of use.
- Create an interface between model and end user by utilizing Excel's dialog box facility.

INTRODUCTION

In the development of a structured spreadsheet model there may be a clear need to automate some or all of the model's operations. A spreadsheet operation may be automated by the construction of a *macro*. A macro is a set of (related) instructions which can be invoked automatically by a single keystroke. The macro may be used to automate a combination of spreadsheet menu commands and specialist built-in functions. The degree of automation required will vary from model to model and will be dependent upon the complexity of the mathematical statements, the degree of end user involvement required and the end user's knowledge of spreadsheet operations.

This chapter describes the approach taken in developing and utilizing macros within a spreadsheet model. The macros considered form part of the simple 'contractor's' model developed using Excel (version 4). While macro development may vary between spreadsheets, the concepts described will be readily transferable to other spreadsheets and modelling applications. Before describing this approach, let us consider the advantages and disadvantages of macro automation.

Advantages of using macros

There are certain advantages in automating a spreadsheet model:

- Automation can ensure that certain operations may be performed without corrupting the model code.
- Automation, supported by comprehensive documentation, facilitates thorough and efficient use of the model.
- In the case of complex models, automation permits their use by a model user with little or no knowledge of either spreadsheet operations or the mathematics which underpins the spreadsheet code.
- As a *minimum*, macros can be used to facilitate the efficient navigation to each block in the structured model.
- For a given application, the (mathematical) capabilities of the spreadsheet may be insufficient. In such situations, macros may be applied as a programming language in a manner analogous to a high-level language such as Fortran. Moreover, this type of application may be unavoidable, since the output generated may form part of the model solution.

Disadvantages of using macros

There are a number of disadvantages in automating a spreadsheet model:

- If the automation of a model is not properly planned, the spreadsheet may lose a degree of its informality, which is seen by many as its most important feature. Reducing the spreadsheet's informality and the opportunity for end-user intervention can limit experimentation and perhaps deter a number of end users from taking advantage of the model.
- Total automation may remove the opportunity for the end user to undertake 'what if' analysis.
- In certain situations, it may be unwise to automate too much of the modelling process. The decision process represented by the model may be more complicated than assumed and this degree of complication may be best approached by ad-hoc end-user intervention.

STAGES IN MACRO DEVELOPMENT

Irrespective of the spreadsheet used, there are a number of important stages to be undertaken in the construction of a macro:

1. Before any macro code is written, the modeller should be able to describe and understand its role within the model. Firstly, the modeller needs to decide whether the macro is necessary. In making this decision, the modeller must be aware of the trade-off between the advantages of automating a spreadsheet routine and the potential loss of informality and experimentation.
2. The writing of the macro code. The best approach to adopt is similar to that employed in coding complex formulae. That is, it may be useful to separate the macro code into short, related sections. This aids end-user understanding and also helps to simplify the debugging

and validation process. Writing macro code in Excel is greatly simplified by using the Record Macro facility which permits the modeller to record each keystroke required in a particular routine and, as a result, can help to minimize mistakes.

3. Macro debugging and validation. For more complicated macro code, the volume of debugging is likely to increase. In validating the macro, the modeller must ensure that the code, when invoked, performs exactly as required.

4. Once the code has been validated it should be properly documented. This documentation must include the macro name, the code and a *full* description of each part of the automated operation. In particular, if the macro code is housed in more than one row of the spreadsheet (which will usually be the case), then each separate row should be appropriately documented.

5. The final stage of macro development involves the modeller determining how appropriate it may be for the macros to be activated manually or invoked using macro buttons. Again, the size and complexity of the model in addition to the informality required by the end user will determine the suitability of constructing macro buttons.

In the development of the 'contractor's' model, an assumption has been made that the end user has no experience of spreadsheet operations. While the model's contents (described in Chapter 4) are simple and the number of end-user operations are small, the modeller has decided to automate the following operations:

- *User support facilities*, which consist of efficient navigation to each self-contained block in the model and a facility which ensures that the introduction screen is activated on model retrieval
- *Functional operations*, which include an input routine, a routine for printing the model's results and facilities for saving the model and quitting the spreadsheet

Finally, to counter the end user's lack of spreadsheet training, the routines which automate all of the facilities described above will be activated in the formal model by assigning macro buttons. Assigning and using macro buttons is described fully later in the chapter.

The development of macro code is arguably that area of the modelling process which is most 'spreadsheet-specific'. That is, the process of writing, testing, and executing a macro will vary (perhaps considerably) from spreadsheet to spreadsheet. In order to keep the contents of this chapter as general as possible, the 'mechanics' of this process will be described; as a result, this chapter is arguably Excel-specific. Once a description of how to create a macro using Excel has been provided, three categories of macro will be defined (in general terms), and by reference to the 'contractor's' model, their role within a formal spreadsheet model will be described.

Additionally, the importance of on-screen macro documentation will be addressed, with reference to the macros written for the 'contractor's' model. At the end of the chapter, a macro facility called the dialog box will be described and it will be demonstrated how this application can be used to provide an interface between a formal model and its end user. Specifically, this will be used in the simple model to ensure that reasonable values are entered for each of the model's parameters: building length, height, width, plus the number of doors and windows.

WRITING A MACRO (in Microsoft Excel)

In Microsoft Excel, two types of macro can be used, namely command macros and function macros. Command macros are generally used to automate repetitive spreadsheet operations (such as saving a model or printing its results screen) and activate user/computer interfaces (dialog boxes) which can be used for processes such as inputting a model's input parameters. This chapter will consider command macros in detail. In contrast, function macros are used to permit a model user to access mathematical formula from a macro sheet, which, once written, may be referenced from any formal model.

To write a simple command macro, Excel's macro recorder can be used. Using this facility, user activities such as selecting menu choices, using the mouse and performing specific keystrokes are recorded. Once these connected activities are validated by the modeller, they can be re-issued by a simple keystroke.

As suggested in Chapter 4, macros are produced on a document separate from the model to which they are assigned. These separate documents are called *macro sheets*. Since the macro code can appear complex, especially for those model users with limited computer experience, and for large applications the volume of code may be large, the advantage of housing the macros on their own spreadsheet should be obvious. In appearance, the macro sheet resembles an ordinary Excel spreadsheet, except that it is assigned the extension .XLM instead of .XLS. Depending upon the size of the particular formal model, most if not all macros (subject to volume of code) can be written and stored on a single macro sheet.

Before recording any macro using Excel, the modeller must open the spreadsheet, in this case **PAINT.XLS**. To record the macro, the modeller must select:

M̲acro
Rec̲ord

and, by doing this, a Record Macro dialog box appears. The Record Macro dialog box is shown in Figure 5.1.

This box requests a suitable name for the macro. Suppose the modeller wishes to record a macro which, when issued, automatically prints the model's results screen. In this case, a name such as PRINT_RESULTS could be used. Each macro used by an Excel model should be saved using a different name. This name must start with a letter and may consist of letters, underscores (_), full stops and numbers but not spaces. The macro name can consist of up to 255 characters and is not case-sensitive.

Once the name has been selected, the modeller needs to press the **TAB** key to activate the Key box, and enter a letter, in this case **p**. By doing this, the modeller has assigned the keystrokes

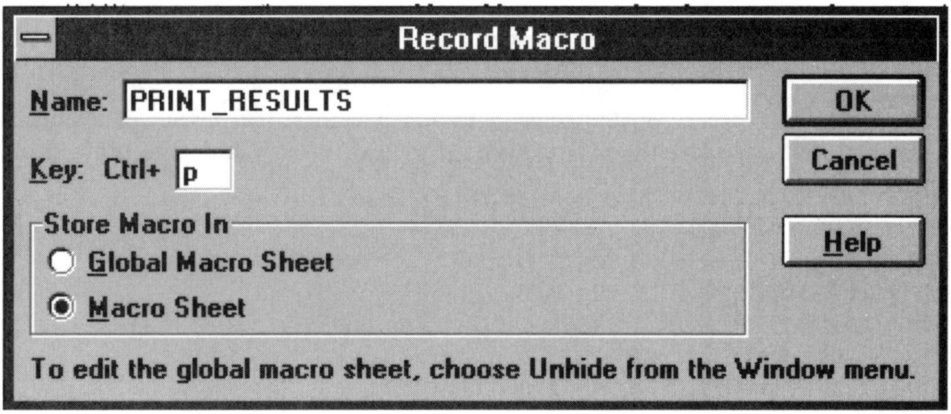

Figure 5.1 Excel's Record Macro dialog box

CTRL-p to run the macro PRINT_RESULTS. It is important to note that the macro key *is* case-sensitive, i.e. **CTRL-p** is different from **CTRL-P**.

Users of Excel 4 are provided with an additional facility called the **Global Macro Sheet**. This particular macro sheet is opened every time Excel is retrieved, and as a consequence, it can be used to run macros common to most or all of an end user's Excel models. The option **Macro Sheet** (which is being considered in this chapter) has to be opened every time the corresponding model is accessed, and as a result should only contain those macros which are specific to a particular application.

Once the macro name and short-key code have been defined, the modeller should click **OK**. This results in a recording message appearing at the bottom of the screen and the modeller can begin to record all of the required menu options and keystrokes.

For the print macro, three keystrokes must be recorded:

- Selection of the results screen
- Setting the print area
- Printing the selected area

To record these keystrokes, the modeller must highlight the appropriate screen in the model and then select:

Options
Set Print Area

Once this has been achieved, the modeller must activate:

File
Print

to define how the results are to be printed (e.g. portrait or landscape, with or without gridlines, number of copies etc), followed by **OK**.

The macro recording is now complete. To stop recording any further keystrokes, the modeller must now select:

Macro
Stop Recorder

In order to view the recorded macro on its macro sheet, the modeller must activate:

Window
Macro1

The macro sheet now appears on the screen. As stated earlier, this resembles a normal spreadsheet, except that once saved it will be assigned the extension .XLM. The print macro has been listed in Figure 5.2.

```
PRINT_RESULTS(p)
=SELECT("R96C46:R113C54")
=SET.PRINT.AREA()
=PRINT(1,,,1,FALSE,FALSE,1,,,300)
=RETURN()
```

Figure 5.2 Print macro written using the Record Macro facility

The recorded macro consists of five lines on the spreadsheet. The first consists of the macro name and its short-key code, i.e. PRINT_RESULTS and **p**. The remaining four lines contain the special macro functions pertaining to the recorded keystrokes, i.e. **SELECT()**, **SET.PRINT.AREA()**, **PRINT()** and **RETURN()**. The appearance of these functions is similar to spreadsheet functions, i.e. they begin with = and end with ( ). The function **RETURN()** signifies the end of the macro. Therefore, any Excel macro always starts with the assigned name and ends with **RETURN()**.

It is worth noting from Figure 5.2 that Excel uses the R1C1 method of defining cells and cell blocks rather than using the column and row letter numbers. As a consequence, it is better to use names for cells and blocks instead. This makes documentation easier and helps facilitate user understanding of the macro's role. In the print macro above, it should be obvious that:

$$= SELECT("res\_screen")$$

is easier to read than:

$$= SELECT("R96C46:R113C54")$$

Moreover, when writing a macro in this way, the modeller should try as best as possible to avoid recording unwanted and unnecessary keystrokes. For example, in the print macro under consideration, the modeller may record the movement of the cursor to the print screen. When the macro is to be issued by the model user, the corresponding command is unnecessary. As a consequence, it should be deleted manually from the macro code, using the appropriate Excel commands (e.g. **Edit Clear**).

Now that the print macro is written, it can be activated by holding down the control (**CTRL**) and assigned letter (**p**) keys simultaneously.

When all of the required macros are written and tested for a particular modelling application, the macro sheet must be saved. Saving, opening, closing and editing (as mentioned above) an Excel macro worksheet is achieved in exactly the same way as for a normal (model) spreadsheet. However, if the model is opened at a later date, and the end user wishes to activate the PRINT_RESULTS macro, simply pressing the **CTRL** and **p** keys will not work. The macro sheet must be opened, in addition to the corresponding model sheet. Version 4 of Microsoft Excel offers a useful facility for opening all required spreadsheets at the same time. This facility is called the *workbook*.

CREATING A WORKBOOK IN EXCEL

In a formal spreadsheet model created using EXCEL, the actual application is likely to consist of a model sheet and one or more associated macro sheets. To ensure that the macro sheets can be opened automatically on retrieval of the corresponding model, version 4 of Excel permits the user to create a single application (consisting of the relevant component parts) which is called a workbook. Equally, once a workbook has been created, it may also be saved as one spreadsheet operation. Moreover, an individual sheet or document can be saved in more than one workbook, (this is likely to be the case for certain macro sheets) and, if required, can be opened as an individual document.

In the 'contractor's' example, the workbook will consist of two documents: the model sheet **PAINT.XLS** and the macro sheet **MACROSHT.XLM**. In addition to the model sheets and macro sheets, other documents which can be added to a workbook in this way are charts. To set up the workbook for the contractor's model, both of these related documents need to be opened. Once this has been done, the modeller must activate:

<u>Window</u>
<u>Arrange</u>

and select the **Tiled** view. Once this has been done, the workbook should be saved by selecting:

<u>File</u>
<u>Save Workbook</u>

followed by **PAINT**. By doing this, the workbook **PAINT.XLW** is created. It should be apparent that where the model has a .XLS extension and the macro sheet a .XLM one, the workbook is given a .XLW extension. When the workbook is opened, all of the related sheets are automatically opened and the contents page of the workbook is displayed. For the 'contractor's' model, this contents page is displayed in Figure 5.3. Moreover, the documents included in the workbook can be either *bound* (i.e. the sheets may form part of one workbook) or unbound (i.e. the separate sheets may form part of more than one workbook, especially macrosheets containing certain generic code).

In order to move around the workbook, the special buttons displayed at the bottom right-hand corner of each page can be used. These buttons are shown in Figure 5.4. The first button allows the user to access the workbook's contents page, the second allows access to the previous document and the last one access to the next document. Finally, it may be necessary to add or remove certain sheets or charts from the workbook. In order to do this, the modeller can simply

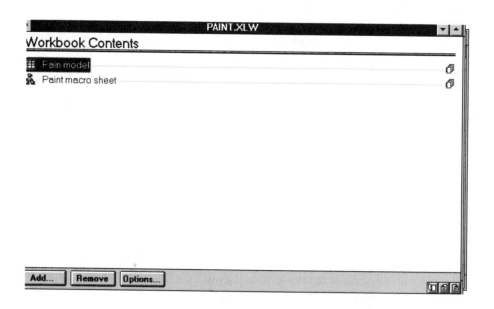

Figure 5.3   Contents page from an Excel workbook

Figure 5.4   Buttons for navigating around an Excel workbook

activate the relevant buttons located in the left-hand corner of the workbook scene, as shown in Figure 5.3.

MACRO WORDS

As described already in this chapter, a set of related macro words can be recorded and activated using a simple key command. For those modellers with limited experience of using macros, the easiest way to write the necessary macro is by exploiting the Record Macro facility. However, simple macros can be added to the macro sheet manually. In the 'contractor's' model, a simple macro:

$$=\textbf{SAVE()}$$
$$=\textbf{RETURN()}$$

can easily be written manually and issued whenever the model user wishes to save the updated model. However, for larger and complex macros, the Record Macro facility should be used, or, if required, a mixture of Record Macro and manual macro development. This will be addressed later in the chapter, by reference to a more complex macro in the 'contractor's' model.

To complement the facilities of the macro recorder, a number of macro words are offered by Excel which can be added to the sections of macro code to provide the modeller (and in turn the model user) with greater power and control over a model than simply recording key commands. Figure 5.5 lists a set of useful (but not exhaustive) macro commands.

DEBUGGING A MACRO

It is likely for those modellers dealing with non-trivial applications of macros, in particular when the code is developed manually rather than using the Record Macro facility, that bugs may occur in the resultant macro code. Obviously, this macro code must be edited in order to achieve the desired results. Use of a macro record facility offered by a number of spreadsheets is useful in that the required keystrokes and menu options can be recorded in such a way that any potential bugs in the resultant code are eliminated. However, when a macro is recorded manually or semi-manually, there is obviously more potential for mistakes to be made. Common mistakes include:

- Incorrect spelling of macro words
- Missing **=RETURN()** at the end of a macro routine
- Missing **=** and **()** at the beginning and end of the macro words

Command	Action
SELECT	Select a cell or range of cells
HLINE, VLINE **HPAGE, VPAGE** **HSCROLL, VSCROLL**	Navigate around the spreadsheet
INPUT, FORMULA	Enter values from the keyboard
FOR, WHILE, NEXT	Repeat a set of macro commands
IF, INPUT, TYPE	Check entered data or decision made

Figure 5.5 Macro commands offered by Excel

Once the bugs have been identified, the modeller must edit the macro code and correct the problem syntax. Re-issuing the macro will indicate whether these problems have been rectified.

CATEGORIES OF MACRO

So far this chapter has described the advantages and disadvantages of automating a spreadsheet model and has considered the development of the simple print macro which will be activated by users of the 'contractor's' model. The next part of the chapter describes in general terms three different categories of command macro which exist and their role within a structured spreadsheet model. The three categories of command macro are defined here as:

- Auto_Open (and Auto_Close) macros
- Navigational macros
- Operational macros

The content and role of the three types of macro will be described by making reference to the simple model. Although this model is written using Excel, the concepts described can be readily applied by modellers using other spreadsheets offering analogous facilities.

Auto_Open and Auto_Close macros

The Auto_Open macro is the macro which is executed automatically on retrieval of the spreadsheet model. In Excel more than one Auto_Open macro can exist, as long as each Auto_Open macro begins with Auto_Open in the name. When a model is retrieved, Excel will identify if any Auto_Open macros exist, and, if so, they will be activated.

If this macro contains bugs, then its (automatic) execution may obviously cause problems. Potential problems can be avoided if the code contained in the Auto_Open macro is kept as simple as possible.

Specifically, this can be achieved by avoiding the functional areas of data input, process and output. In practice, an Auto_Open macro is best employed in defining the presentation of the model on retrieval. The factors accounted for may include the position of the cursor on model retrieval and removal of borders to enhance the model's appearance (see Chapter 9). The Auto_Open macro written for the 'contractor's' model using the Record Macro facility is shown in Figure 5.6.

This macro instructs the spreadsheet on retrieval to move to cell A1 (by issuing =FORMULA.GOTO("R1C1")), suppress the row and column borders and remove the gridlines (=DISPLAY(FALSE,FALSE,FALSE,TRUE,0,,TRUE,FALSE,1)) and define the size of the window (=WINDOW.SIZE(491.25,287.25)), so that each screen used in the model structure fits exactly onto the PC screen. This is a useful macro to execute on model retrieval, because it locates the cursor at the top left-hand corner of the introduction screen (one of the

```
Auto_Open
=FORMULA.GOTO("R1C1")
=DISPLAY(FALSE,FALSE,FALSE,TRUE,0,,TRUE,FALSE,1)
=WINDOW.SIZE(491.25,287.25)
=RETURN()
```

Figure 5.6   An Auto_Open macro written in Excel

requirements listed earlier in the chapter). Removing row and column borders and gridlines is useful because the appearance of the spreadsheet becomes more user-friendly.

Moreover, viewing the introduction screen(s) on model retrieval promotes a friendly environment since the end user is provided with an on-screen explanation of the model. In short, the commands invoked by this Auto_Open macro are far more preferable to executing a data entry procedure directly on the retrieval of the model.

Using the same logic, any macro starting with Auto_Close will be activated once the spreadsheet housing the model is to be closed. Again, commands influencing the input, process and output of data should be avoided when writing this type of macro. Typically, the Auto_Close macro should be used to undertake operations such as saving an updated model to disk.

Navigational macros

One essential feature of a user-friendly spreadsheet model is the provision of a facility which allows a model user to move from block to block efficiently within the model. If the model employs a block structure similar to that described in Chapter 3, then this ease of movement can be facilitated by invoking an appropriate *navigational macro*. In practice, a navigational macro written in Excel will consist of related **GOTO** and **SELECT** statements.

If a block structure has been employed like that illustrated in Figure 3.4, the modeller should recognize that the model user may wish to navigate to a particular block either from a position above and to the left or a position below and to the right of the required block.

The simplest way to record a navigational macro is to ensure that each screen used in the block structure has been named. In the 'contractor's' model, the results screen has been named res_screen. Using the Record Macro facility, the modeller should first record pressing the **F5** (Goto) key and selecting the appropriate screen. By doing this, the whole screen is highlighted as shown in Figure 5.7.

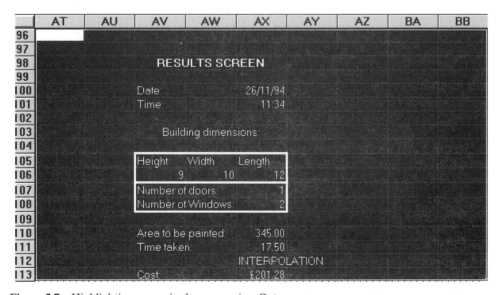

Figure 5.7 Highlighting a required screen using **Goto**

```
=FORMULA.GOTO("res_screen")
=SELECT("R96C46")
=RETURN()
```

Figure 5.8   Navigational macro written for an Excel model

Obviously, the model user would not wish for the whole screen to be highlighted when the navigational macro is activated. The next part of the macro routine should be to select the cell in the top left-hand corner of the block. This may be achieved by pointing to the required cell and clicking the mouse. Moreover, by combining these two commands, the resultant macro can be used to navigate to the required screen from anywhere within the formal model structure. The navigational macro corresponding to the results screen is presented in Figure 5.8.

Operational macros

Operational macros are those sections of spreadsheet code which deal with automating certain routines within the functional areas of input, process and output of data. In the 'contractor's' model, there are four operational macros: an input routine, a facility for printing the model's results and facilities for saving and quitting the model. However, it should be obvious that the volume and complexity of the operational macros used in a formal model will be influenced by the difficulty of the modelling situation and the degree of automation required by the end user. The print macro used in the 'contractor's' model is illustrated in Figure 5.2. This macro is simple since it consists of a routine which activates a spreadsheet's menu option. In contrast, the input routine illustrated in Figure 5.15 represents a more complex operational macro.

In reality, a proportion of time taken in the development of an operational macro should be spent away from the spreadsheet. This time may include considering the conceptual model identifying the relationships between variables and determining the possible values of each variables. These considerations must be addressed before deriving the mathematical relationships which form the basis of the spreadsheet code.

In determining the appropriate degree of automation, the modeller must take into account a number of factors:

- The complexity of the mathematical model and the mathematical ability of the end user. Even the simplest of models may have to be fully automated for a non-numerate model user with little experience of spreadsheets. The 'contractor's' model represents an example when all model operations need to be automated.
- 'Messy' mathematical problems might not be represented exactly by a particular modelling technique. Moreover, any differences may have to be accounted for by end-user intervention. A fully automated model may not permit this combination of judgemental and quantitative analysis.
- Certain business problems require a degree of 'what if' analysis, whereby the end user is required to determine the effect of changing the values of one or parameters in the business model. In such a situation, the modeller should be aware of the trade-off between automation and experimentation, but, if possible, incorporate the use of certain modelling facilities within a fully automated spreadsheet model.

- A number of model users will be spreadsheet literate and may value the informality that the spreadsheet offers. Such users may require only minimal model automation.

MACRO DOCUMENTATION

In general, the spreadsheet model may at some time have to be updated to account for changes in the business process. To facilitate straightforward understanding, the operational macros should be well structured and documented. Additionally, the presentation of macro code is also very important. These issues are illustrated below by considering the print macro incorporated in the 'contractor's' model. Figure 5.9 shows two possible ways of presenting this macro.

In both cases, the same actions will be performed, i.e. printing the results screen. However, even the most inexperienced of spreadsheet modellers will notice that the second block of code is easier to understand. In developing both print macros, the spreadsheet code has been broken down into small, related parts. This facilitates end-user understanding and, for more complicated macros, will simplify the validation and debugging process. In short, it is good practice, even for simple operational macros, to break the macro code into short, related sections. This is done automatically in Excel by using the spreadsheet's Record Macro facility.

Additionally, there may be situations which require operational macros to incorporate formulae and built-in menu commands (such as **Printing the results screen** in the Excel model). In both situations, it is good practice to utilize range and cell names in the macro code, as utilized in the second macro. This can ensure that any changes to the model structure, in particular addition or deletion of screens within any of the model's blocks, will not affect the operation of a particular macro. Moreover, a modeller may prefer to distinguish between menu commands and range names or cell references when constructing macro code. This has been achieved for the print macro in Figure 5.9 because the spreadsheet's keystrokes are in upper case (the Excel default), while the range names are in lower case.

The second and perhaps the most important reason why the second macro is much better presented is that each line of macro code is accompanied by a comment describing its role. In general, any section of macro code, simple or complex, should be properly documented. Although the issue of model documentation is described fully in Chapter 7, documentation of macro code will also be considered in this chapter. Documentation of macro code is vital, but many modellers wrongly believe the spreadsheet to be self-documenting. This is primarily because of the 'informal' approach to computing and modelling permitted by the spreadsheet.

```
PRINT_RESULTS(p)
=SELECT("R96C46:R113C54")
=SET.PRINT.AREA()                        print macro
=PRINT(1,,,1,FALSE,FALSE,1,,,300)
=RETURN()
```

```
PRINT_RESULTS(p)                         print macro – print results
=SELECT("res_screen")                    results screen highlighted
=SET.PRINT.AREA()                        print area defined as above
=PRINT(1,,,1,FALSE,FALSE,1,,,300)        print option selected (default)
=RETURN()                                end of macro
```

Figure 5.9 Comparing the presentation of two equivalent macros

Lotus 1-2-3 code

```
{calc}
/pp
rOUTPUT~
g
q
```

Excel code

```
PRINT_RESULTS(p)
=SELECT("res_screen")
=SET.PRINT.AREA()
=PRINT(1,,,1,FALSE,FALSE,1,,,300)
=RETURN()
```

Figure 5.10   Comparison of spreadsheet macro code

However, the lack of self-documentation offered by certain spreadsheets is clearly evident when comparing the macro code with its equivalent written in a high-level programming language such as Fortran. Figure 5.10 compares the print macro from the 'contractor's' model written using Excel with an analogous statement written using Lotus 1-2-3.

The Excel code is much easier to follow than its equivalent code in Lotus 1-2-3 because it uses quasi-English statements. In contrast, the Lotus code is less straightforward to understand, especially for a model user with limited knowledge of spreadsheet operations. Nevertheless, it is vital to provide detailed documentation to support the use of all macros, even those written in Excel, since this documentation not only facilitates end-user understanding, but provides the necessary support to those responsible for maintaining the model.

A useful method of macro documentation involves utilizing a two-column format, where the first column contains the macro name and key code as title with the corresponding code located beneath it, and the second column contains the detailed line-by-line documentation. Most operational macros will generally extend to more than one row of the spreadsheet, and as a consequence, *each row* should contain comprehensive documentation. In non-trivial applications, a brief overview of a macro's role may be of little use. As stated, it is useful to consider the simple print macro used in the 'contractor's' model. Figure 5.9 illustrated two possible ways of documenting this macro, one with a line-by-line description and the other where the documentation is restricted to a single comment.

In general, most formal models will contain a range of macros (if only to facilitate user navigation). One useful way to arrange a suite of macros on the macro sheet is by housing the macro code in column A and the corresponding line-by-line description in column B with an empty row between each individual section of macro code. This makes the macro sheet easy to read and maintain. Moreover, a list of range names could be generated and housed as a summary, perhaps at the foot of the macro sheet.

For macros which are more complex than the simple print macro described, a single line overview is likely to be of little value, especially to those who will be responsible for updating or maintaining the model. Using the two-column arrangement described above, there is sufficient space to house the required documentation and, since the macro code is housed on its own self-contained sheet, potentially large volumes of macro code and associated documentation will not affect the structure and layout of the actual spreadsheet model.

In terms of producing macro documentation, this is best undertaken hand-in-hand with the construction of the macro code. Before writing any spreadsheet code, it is good practice for the modeller to write in English the intended use of the code. This can be used as a basis for both spreadsheet and external documentation. As each section of macro code is written and/or recorded, this initial documentation can be refined and expanded until a thorough explanation has been produced similar to that illustrated in Figure 5.9.

The two-column structure illustrated is neat and makes the macro code easy to read. If a modeller is catering for an end user with little or no spreadsheet training, it may be appropriate to activate the model's macros using assigned macro buttons rather than the keystrokes described earlier in the chapter. Macro buttons will be discussed shortly.

FUNCTION MACROS

Excel contains a large number of mathematical, statistical and financial functions which may be used within a formal business model or solely to perform one-off calculations. Examples of this type of function were the statistical measures listed in Chapter 2. These functions may be specified on a spreadsheet when required by the spreadsheet user either by typing in the required function or by pasting it into the appropriate cell. However, there will be situations when these functions individually may not solve a particular problem. In those instances when a particular function will be used repeatedly, perhaps by different personnel on a number of spreadsheets, it may prove useful for the modeller to write a function macro, which will be stored on a macro sheet.

For example, the area of building to be painted is given by the formula:

$$AREA = 2*HEIGHT*(LENGTH + WIDTH)-((21*DOORS)+(15*WINDOWS))$$

The macro corresponding to this formula is given in Figure 5.11.

AREA
= RESULT(1)
= ARGUMENT("Height",1)
= ARGUMENT("Length",1)
= ARGUMENT("Width",1)
= ARGUMENT("Doors",1)
= ARGUMENT("Windows",1)
= 2*Height*(Length + Width)−((21*Doors)+(15*Windows))
= RETURN(L51)

Figure 5.11 Function macro written in Excel

The name at the top of the macro code, **AREA**, is the function name and is defined as such by the modeller activating:

Formula
<u>D</u>efine Name

and by doing this the macro is specified as a function. The next line, **= RESULT(1)**, specifies the type of result generated by the macro function, i.e. a number. In general, the types of results and arguments used in the function macro are:

1	Number	8	Reference
2	Text	16	Error
4	Logical	64	Array

The next five lines in the function code defines the five model parameters as function variables. These variables are known as 'arguments' and must be defined in a macro function before being used in any formulae. The structure of the argument statement is:

ARGUMENT(Name of Argument, Type of Argument)

where the name is provided in double quotes and should not contain spaces. For example, Height is specified by the argument statement:

= ARGUMENT("Height",1)

i.e. variable 'Height' is entered into the formula as a number. Finally, the last statement in the function:

= RETURN(L51)

signifies the end of the function macro and also indicates the position within the model to where the calculation will be entered, i.e. cell L51. Again, this type of macro should be documented using the two-column arrangement described earlier in the chapter.

When the function macro has been written, it will be saved on a macro sheet, preferably one containing functions only. To activate the function, the following type of formula should be written by the modeller:

=MACRO FILENAME! MACRO NAME(Arg1, Arg2, Arg3, etc.)

In this example, if the function has been saved to a macro sheet called **FUNC.XLM**, the formula entered into the spreadsheet model would be:

= FUNC.XLM!AREA(12,10,10,2,1)

where the numbers in the bracket refer to the dimensions of a particular building. If the formula is to be used in a formal business model, cell names or references may be used instead of values for each argument defined.

ASSIGNING BUTTONS TO MACROS

For each macro described in this chapter, activation may be achieved by holding down the control (**CTRL**) and assigned letter key simultaneously. For example, **CTRL-p** will activate the print macro used in the 'contractor's' model.

However, for a number of model users, especially those with limited spreadsheet experience, even this may prove troublesome. The process of activating the required macro can, however, be further simplified by assigning buttons to each macro within a formal business model. Once a macro is assigned to a button, the end user simply has to click on the button (which will be located in an appropriate place within the formal model structure), and the macro will be issued. To create a button, the modeller needs to click the button tool which is located on Excel's Utility toolbar. This is shown in Figure 5.12.

Once activated, the modeller should position and size the button (by pointing and dragging with the mouse) in the appropriate place in the model. By releasing the mouse button, the macro button will be in place and will contain the default name '**Button**'.

(macro button)

Figure 5.12 Utility toolbar in Excel

To assign a macro to a particular button, the required macro is simply selected by name from the Assign to Object dialog box which is opened automatically by Excel. In a formal model structure, certain navigational macros may be assigned to two or more buttons, and this is allowable in Excel.

The next step is to assign a relevant name to the button and, if required, customize its appearance to fit in with the spreadsheet model. To do this, the modeller must first select it by holding down the **CTRL** key and clicking on the button. The **CTRL** key has to be pressed so that the assigned macro is not activated. Text can be erased in the normal way and replaced with a relevant name, such as '**Input Data**' or '**Print**'.

One important aspect the reader should note about a macro button is that its location within the formal model is fixed. That is, if a button has been assigned to the print macro and is located in the results screen, it will not be on the screen if the end user navigates, say, to the model's input block or introductory screen. As a result, careful planning is required as to the location of each button within a model structure. In the 'contractor's' example, it was considered appropriate to have a button name '**Intro**' located on each block accessed by the model user, and, obviously, these buttons are assigned to the same macro. Figure 5.13 pictures the input screen, which houses two macro buttons.

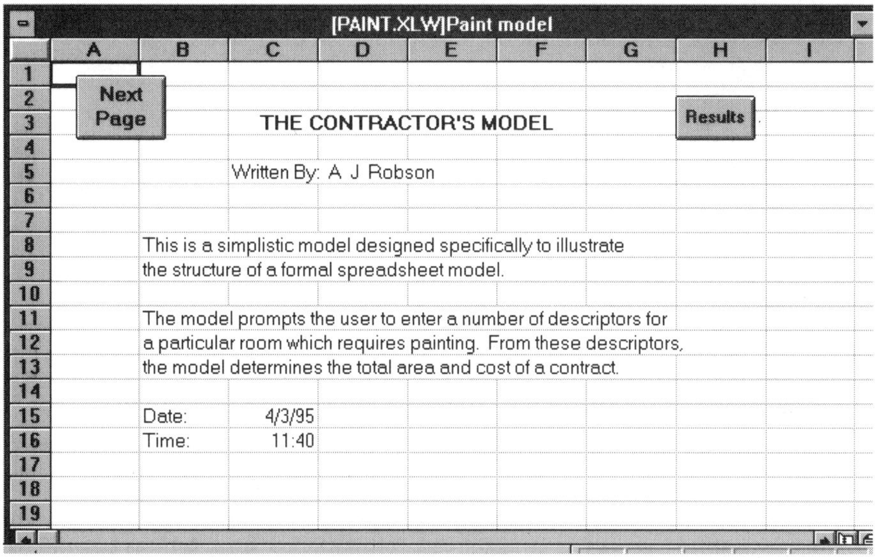

	A	B	C	D	E	F	G	H	I
				[PAINT.XLW]Paint model					
1									
2		Next							
3		Page		THE CONTRACTOR'S MODEL				Results	
4									
5			Written By: A J Robson						
6									
7									
8		This is a simplistic model designed specifically to illustrate							
9		the structure of a formal spreadsheet model.							
10									
11		The model prompts the user to enter a number of descriptors for							
12		a particular room which requires painting. From these descriptors,							
13		the model determines the total area and cost of a contract.							
14									
15		Date:	4/3/95						
16		Time:	11:40						
17									
18									
19									

Figure 5.13 'Contractor's' model housing macro buttons

Finally, to activate a macro using the button, the model user simply has to point to the button. By doing this a hand appears. By clicking on the mouse, the assigned macro will then be issued.

CREATING A USER–COMPUTER INTERFACE USING A DIALOG BOX

If a formal spreadsheet model is to be used by personnel with limited spreadsheet experience, it may be useful to control the values of input variables used within a formal model. For example, in the 'contractor's' model, the following controls must be placed on the dimensions of the building under consideration:

Length Number > 0
Height Number > 0
Width Number > 0
Doors Integer > 0
Windows Integer > 0

For any contract under consideration, these values must be input by the model user, from which contract duration and cost are determined. Therefore, the formal model requires a user interface which serves two purposes:

- It is user-friendly in appearance and easy to activate for an end user with limited knowledge of Excel.
- It ensures that only reasonable (as defined above) values can be input for each parameter.

To build this interface, an Excel facility called a *dialog box* will be used. Once this interface is written and defined, it will then be activated (via a macro button) using an appropriate macro routine.

To activate the dialog box facility, the modeller must open the workbook containing the model and macro sheet (i.e. **PAINT.XLS** for the contractor's model), click on the control menu icon (the grey box in the top left-hand corner of the macro sheet) and select:

Run

from the application menu bar, followed by **Dialog Editor**. This editor has three menus, namely **File**, **Edit** and **Item**.

At this stage, the border of the new dialog box appears on the spreadsheet screen. By clicking and dragging on the mouse, the position and size of the box can be defined. This box is shown in Figure 5.14.

From the **Item** menu, the modeller can select **Button** to define the buttons used in this box. In the dialog box for the 'contractor's' model, two buttons are defined, namely **OK** and **Cancel**.

The second facility which may be selected from the **Item** menu is **Text**. On selection, this produces a feint box incorporating the word 'Text' which may be edited or overtyped. Such boxes are used in this dialog box for each of the model's parameters, namely length, height, width, doors and windows.

For each of the parameters listed above, **Edit boxes** are specified from the **Item** menu. These edit boxes are particularly useful because the modeller can define the type of data to be input by the user. Five choices are provided: Text, Integer, Number, Formula or Reference. In the 'contractor's' model, the edit boxes for length, height and width are defined as number, while those corresponding to doors and windows are defined as integer.

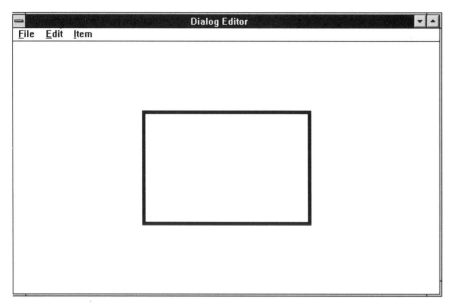

Figure 5.14   Excel's dialog editor

Once the dialog box has been defined in this way, the corresponding data should be transferred to a macro sheet by selecting:

Edit
Select All

followed by:

Edit
Copy

At this stage, the modeller will have copied the information to the clipboard. By closing the Dialog Editor and opening a macro sheet, (perhaps macro sheet defined specifically for dialog boxes), the dialog box information can be stored at an appropriate location by activating:

Edit
Paste

The table of data corresponding to the dialog box developed for the 'contractor's' model is displayed in Figure 5.15.

The data corresponding to this dialog box consists of seven columns which house the following information:

1   A code number for each item defined within the dialog box, the items being **OK** and **Cancel** buttons, text, text boxes, numbers, number boxes, etc.
2   The X coordinate for an item's position
3   The Y coordinate for an item's position
4   The item's width
5   The item's height

D	E	F	G	H	I	J
			230	268	Paint model	
5	10	6			Input relevant information:	
5	10	24			Length of building:	
8	10	39	160			12
5	10	63			Height of building:	
8	10	78	160			10
5	10	102			Width of building:	
8	10	117	160			10
5	10	141			Number of windows:	
7	10	156	160			1
5	10	180			Number of doors:	
7	10	195	160			1
1	10	216	88		OK	
2	10	240	88		Cancel	

Figure 5.15   Dialog box details stored on macro sheet

The dimensions in 2 to 5 inclusive are used to control the size and position of the dialog box relative to screen units.

6   The text column which specifies the text used inside the various buttons, boxes and groups in the dialog box
7   The results column which indicates the current values of the various items, i.e. length = 12, height = 10, width = 10, windows = 1, and doors = 1. These are the current dimensions of a building under consideration.

Now that the dialog box information has been defined, all of the information listed in the seven columns described above must be named. In this example, the information has been named input_screen because it is used to facilitate the control and input of the model's parameters.

It is important to note that this information must be stored. If it erased, then the dialog box cannot be activated. It should also be apparent that the code generated is not self-documenting. The modeller may find it useful to add column headings (based on the description given above) and a set of supplementary notes either adjacent to or underneath this block of code.

ACTIVATING THE DIALOG BOX

Now that the dialog box has been defined, a macro must be written which activates the corresponding code. In order to activate a dialog box using a macro, the command =DIALOG.BOX() must be used.

In the input routine corresponding to the 'contractor's' model, the following steps must be undertaken as defined by the model user:

- Existing model parameters must be erased
- Their values must be replaced by the model user via a user-friendly interface
- The value of these input parameters must be checked for validity

```
input_macro
=SELECT("R43C23")
=SELECT("R43C23:R51C23")
=CLEAR(3)
=SET.VALUE(length,"")
=SET.VALUE(height,"")
=SET.VALUE(width,"")
=SET.VALUE(windows,"")
=SET.VALUE(doors,"")
=DIALOG.BOX(input_screen)
=WHILE(OR(length < 0,height < 0,width < 0,windows < 0,doors < 0))
=DIALOG.BOX(input_screen)
=NEXT()
=FORMULA(length)
=SELECT("r[2]c")
=FORMULA(height)
=SELECT("r[2]c")
=FORMULA(width)
=SELECT("r[2]c")
=FORMULA(windows)
=SELECT("r[2]c")
=FORMULA(doors)
=RETURN()
```

Figure 5.16   Excel macro which activates the dialog box

The macro which performs these tasks is given in Figure 5.16. This macro was developed using a combination of both manual programming and use of the Record Macro facility.

Erasing the existing model parameters

This is achieved by activating the first three lines of the macro, which were written using the Record Macro facility.

Entering new values

The next part of the macro is involved with the input of the new model parameters. The **SET.VALUE()** command is used to set the initial value of each of the five parameters to zero before the dialog box is activated.

Checking the parameters for validity

The dialog box is then activated using the command =**DIALOG.BOX(input_screen)**. Although the nature of each parameter is fixed using the dialog box, e.g. height as a number, doors as an integer, a further test is incorporated within the input macro to ensure that each parameter is non-negative. This achieved by including a **WHILE()** statement and the logical **OR** function ensures that the dialog box is re-activated if any one of the five parameters is negative.

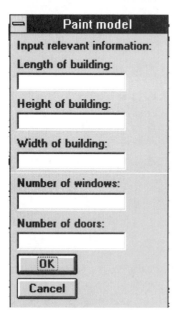

Figure 5.17 Dialog box as it appears on the model screen

Entering the values into the formal model

Once reasonable values have been entered, the **NEXT( )** command transfers the execution of the macro to the next piece of code. The final part of the macro routine ensures that the value of each parameter is written to the appropriate cell within the formal model. **SELECT("r[2]c")** results in the selection of a cell two rows immediately below where the cursor is currently positioned.

Moreover, a button has been assigned to this particular macro, and, when activated, a dialog box resembling that in Figure 5.17 appears on the screen. To enter the data, the model user simply clicks on the appropriate box and enters the value of the building's dimension. If incorrect data is entered (i.e. text or negative or non-integer values), the dialog box stays on the screen until the rogue entries are rectified.

CONCLUSIONS

This chapter has described the issues to be addressed before automating a spreadsheet model. Moreover, a number of advantages and disadvantages in model automation have been identified. The factors affecting the inclusion of macros in a formal model include the modelling situation itself, the flexibility of the spreadsheet, plus the needs and abilities of the model user.

Three types of macro have been defined: Auto_Open (and Auto_Close) macros, navigational macros and operational macros. The Auto_Open macro should be used to define the conditions of the model on retrieval, e.g. suppression of borders and positioning the cursor. More importantly, its code should be kept as simple as possible, and, specifically, avoid the functional areas of the model. The navigational macros facilitate the efficient movement from block to block within the model. Depending on the degree of automation required by the end user, any formal model should contain a minimal degree of automation if only to facilitate this efficient navigation. Finally, operational macros are used to assist in the functional areas of data input, process and output. In practice, these are the most difficult to code and their success will be influenced by the complexity of the modelling situation and the skill of the modeller.

Additionally, the importance of macro documentation and presentation has been emphasized in this chapter. A two-column method of documentation has been suggested, consisting of macro name and code in column A of the macro sheet and a row-by-row explanation of this code housed in an adjacent column.

At the end of the chapter, two user-friendly facilities offered by Excel have been described, again with reference to the simple 'contractor's' model. The first was the concept of assigning buttons to macro code which simplifies their execution for those model users who may be deterred by having to undertake key operations. Once a button is assigned to a macro, the model user simply has to point and click on the button and the assigned routine is automatically carried out.

Finally, the issue of providing a user interface for data entry has been addressed. A user-friendly interface can be built in Excel by using the dialog box facility. This facility can also be used to ensure that the appropriate type of data is entered for each input variable. Moreover, once a dialog box has been defined, a macro routine can be used to activate it, by making use of the **=DIALOG.BOX( )** command.

REVIEW QUESTIONS

1. Describe the reasons for automating either all or part of a spreadsheet model.
2. Define the term 'macro'.
3. Describe the advantages and disadvantages of model automation.
4. Why is it useful to develop a workbook in Excel when a macro sheet has been written to accompany a formal model?
5. Describe the three types of command macro.
6. Outline what *should* and *should not* be included in an Auto_Open or Auto_Close macro.
7. Outline the essential features of the code used in the navigational macros.
8. Describe the factors which must be considered before constructing an operational macro.
9. Why is the spreadsheet code used to construct a macro non-self-documenting?
10. Describe an effective method of macro documentation and presentation.
11. Describe briefly the advantage of using a dialog box as an interface between a formal model and the model user.
12. Why is it useful to assign buttons to macros within a formal model?

CASE STUDY QUESTIONS

1. Create and test an Auto_Open macro which ensures that the introduction screen is accessed immediately on the retrieval of the model, each screen in the model structure consists of the same number of rows and columns and row and column headings and gridlines are removed.
2. Create and test a set of navigational macros which can be used by the end user in order to move easily from block to block within the formal model structure. Use the range names defined in the previous chapter in order to ensure that the macro code is easy to read and understand.
3. Create and test the following operational macros:
   - A macro which can be used to print the results screen automatically
   - A macro which can be used to automatically save the updated model
   - A macro which can be used to exit from the model

In Questions 1, 2 and 3, arrange the macros properly, providing detailed documentation for each macro housed on the macro sheet.

4. For the investment model, construct a suitable user interface using the dialog box facility which will permit the entry of the following input variables:
   - Unit sales in the first year
   - Growth rate per annum (%)
   - Price per unit (£)
   - Cost per unit (£)
   - Interest rate (%)
   - Amount invested (£)

   The input routine should ensure that all of the values entered are numerical rather than textual. With the exception of growth rate, none of the other variables can have negative values. Moreover, growth rate and interest rate must be entered as fractional values.

5. Write a macro which will activate the dialog box designed in Question 4. Moreover, add the appropriate statements to the macro routine which ensure that rogue data values cannot be entered. Again, for Questions 4 and 5, arrange the macros properly, providing documentation for each line of code used in the individual macros. Add appropriate titles and comments to the code pertaining to the dialog box constructed in Question 4.

6. For all of the macros written for this investment model, assign macro buttons.

SIX

MODEL VALIDATION AND VERIFICATION

OVERVIEW

This chapter describes the importance of validation and verification in the development of a structured spreadsheet model. The concepts of validation and verification are introduced, and the iterative nature of the modelling process with respect to model validation and problem conceptualization demonstrated.

OBJECTIVES

After reading this chapter and working through the questions, the reader will be able to:

- Understand the need to validate a spreadsheet model.
- Understand how model validity can be facilitated by the construction of a thorough input routine for a model's parameters.
- Recognize the need to verify the spreadsheet code used within a model.
- Understand the benefits of using 'auditing' facilities to verify the spreadsheet code.
- Understand how the validation and verification process is iterative with respect to data collection and problem conceptualization.

INTRODUCTION

Once a spreadsheet model has been developed, it can be considered as a (model) prototype. The modeller can use this prototype to determine the potential effectiveness (and deficiencies) of the model developed. Moreover, the assumptions made during the modelling process can be tested for thoroughness and, where necessary, modifications can be made to the conceptual model. Additionally, if a block structure has been adopted in the development of the prototype model, then its contents can be easily amended until both the modeller and end user are in agreement with the level of accuracy attained.

Generally, the (spreadsheet) model will be a simplification of reality. For more complex modelling situations, the relative degree of simplification is likely to be greater. The extent of this simplification can be measured by comparing the model's output with that of the actual process under consideration. The level of accuracy attained is an indication of the model's *validity*. This validation process is represented in Figure 6.1.

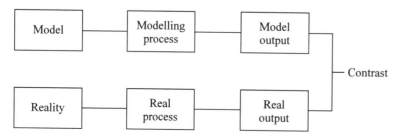

Figure 6.1 Diagrammatical representation of model validation

In short, the validation process is an investigation into how well the model can represent the real process. In other words, a measure of a model's validity is its ability to duplicate known results.

In contrast, verification is the process in which the logic and consistency of the (spreadsheet) code is considered. To verify the model, the modeller must ensure that the spreadsheet code is consistent with the conceptual model developed to represent the business problem.

To illustrate how model validation and verification can be undertaken for a formal spreadsheet model, the 'contractor's' model will be considered. Since the modelling process is simple, the volume of spreadsheet code is relatively small.

MODEL VALIDATION

As described, validation is the process whereby the modeller can determine how accurately the model can duplicate known results. In the contractor's model, the model process involves using a simple linear regression model to describe and predict contract time in terms of size (area) of the building.

As a reminder, this relationship was quantified using the Regression facility provided by Microsoft Excel. In this simple regression equation, the variable of interest, y, was contract time, and the controllable variable, x, was building size.

In short, the validation of the 'contractor's' model involves determining the validity of this simple (regression) model. The process of validating a regression equation is well established and involves the modeller undertaking three tests:

- Testing the overall significance of the regression equation by constructing an appropriate F test
- Testing the significance of the independent variable, namely area, by constructing an appropriate t test
- Undertaking residual (or error) analysis to ensure that the residuals are normally distributed, are independent and are of constant variance

These tests are covered in a number of statistical tests, and in order to ensure that the reader focuses on the modelling concepts, they will not be considered in this chapter.

Moreover, the validation of the regression equation can be performed using either the spreadsheet (either the toolkit or the built-in functions offered by Excel) or a statistical package such as MINITAB. In either case, the analysis and corresponding results should be appropriately documented by the modeller and form part of the model's external or technical documentation. Model documentation is described fully in Chapter 7.

Iterative nature of the modelling process

If the tests on the regression equation indicate either a weak or an invalid relationship between time and area, then the modeller may be required to undertake further conceptualization of the business problem. This additional work may involve identifying other variables which may influence contract time. In identifying extra variables to be considered in the regression equation, the modeller may have to collect additional, appropriate data. In doing so, the modeller has seen how the modelling process can be iterative. That is, the steps in the modelling process, which form the basis of this book, may be interrelated rather than sequential for a non-trivial modelling application.

Moreover, in agreeing the terms of reference with the end user, the modeller may have to develop a model which predicts contract time to a *predetermined* level of accuracy. In such a situation, the model may be treated as a prototype and used to predict the times for a number of selected contracts. Once the actual contracts have been undertaken and their duration measured, the model's accuracy and, in turn, its validity can be assessed.

The other part of the contractor's model which must be tested for validity is the equation which converts the dimensions of a building (the model's input parameters) into area. In particular, this equation assumes that doors and windows are of constant size. Using the model as a prototype in the manner described above, the modeller can record the number of occasions when this assumption is violated. If it is violated frequently, then the standard size of windows and doors hard-coded into the model's equations should be removed and the sizes be input as model parameters in the same way as the building's dimensions.

In general, the method of model validation will be dictated by the size and complexity of the spreadsheet application. Common methods of validation will include:

* Use of electronic calculator for the simpler applications
* Use of statistical packages and other appropriate application software for formal modelling applications. The former would be particularly useful in validating the regression output utilized in this model. However, this method might be limited by software availability and modeller training. In constructing a spreadsheet model for such applications, the author has assumed that the end user is familiar with spreadsheets only
* Use of high-level languages for iterative calculations
* An appropriate combination of the methods described above

Finally, if systematic differences are highlighted between the model's output and reality, then the deviations may be accounted for by introducing changes to the spreadsheet code. Alternatively, further conceptualization of the business problem may be required. Either way, the modeller will have approached the modelling situation in an iterative rather than a sequential manner.

MODEL VERIFICATION

As described in the introduction to this chapter, verification is the process by which the logic and consistency of the (spreadsheet) code is considered. For the contractor's model, there are four main equations to consider:

* The relationship between contract time and size (area). That is, the equation which uses the output from the spreadsheet's regression facility accurately reflects this relationship.
* The calculation of area using the building's dimensions, minus the combined area of the doors and windows.

- The calculation of time for a particular contract using the regression model and computation of area described above. Additionally, the accuracy of the 'interpolation or extrapolation' message should be assessed.
- The calculation of contract costs using the standard rates from the 'lookup' table.

Moreover, it should be apparent to the reader that models of increasing complexity require more complex and time-consuming verification.

In the simple model under consideration, the spreadsheet code is small in volume and non-complex. As a consequence, much of the verification can be undertaken using an electronic calculator. The most complex part of the process in this application is ensuring that the y and x variables have been properly defined in the regression equation. In this model, building size influences contract duration and it can be measured easily by the model user. It therefore represents the independent or x variable. In contrast, *the model user is interested in predicting contract duration*, so time represents the dependent or y variable. As described earlier, any subsequent validation of the results can be performed using a suitable statistics package.

The remainder of the verification involves examining the simple formulae for area, time and cost, and ensuring that they accurately represent the relationships determined from the conceptual model. The conceptual model is shown in Figure 6.2. The labelling used in this model was defined in Chapter 2.

The first part of the conceptual model indicates that the input variables called 'dimension' directly influence the intermediate variable size (building area). To ensure that the spreadsheet code is consistent with this part of the conceptual model, comparison needs to be made with the relevant equation used in the spreadsheet model. The equation used is:

$$\text{AREA} = 2 * \text{HEIGHT} * (\text{LENGTH} + \text{WIDTH}) - ((\text{DOORS} * 21) + (\text{WINDOWS} * 15))$$

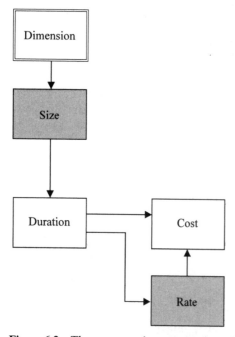

Figure 6.2 The conceptual representation of the 'contractor's' model

and, as required, this indicates that area is influenced by the building's dimensions. The next part of the conceptual model suggests that size influences contract duration. In the spreadsheet model, this relationship is represented by the regression equation:

$$TIME = -1.004 + 0.048 * AREA$$

In turn, the conceptual model suggests that duration influences both contract rate and total cost. To verify the effect of duration on contract rate, the modeller should examine the information housed in the model's 'lookup' table and references made to it by the formula hard-coded into the model. Moreover, the conceptual model suggests that contract rate also influences cost. This is verified after considering the spreadsheet formula:

$$COST = = VLOOKUP() * DURATION$$

where the $=$VTABLE command references the appropriate hourly rate.

TEST DATA TO SUPPORT MODEL VALIDATION AND VERIFICATION

In general, it may be useful for the modeller to design a set of test data to support the validation and verification process. It should be apparent that the testing of a prototype model is of great importance, especially when the model is to be utilized by an end user with limited experience of spreadsheets. Moreover, the factors taken into account in developing such test data may be incorporated into the development of the model's code. In general, there are three categories of data which should be developed:

- Use of inappropriate or unexpected data as input variables. This test data may include negative values or text when positive values are required. This testing will give an indication of the model's strength and its flexibility in dealing with incorrect data entry. A measure of this flexibility is the quality of the error messages or prompts provided by the model.
- Use of simple data to facilitate the verification of each relationship in the spreadsheet model. This simple data allows the comparison of the model output with that produced from hand calculation or electronic calculator. Moreover, any errors in the spreadsheet code can be easily identified.
- Data sets which can be normally associated with the process under consideration. The results of these tests will give a measure of the model's validity, i.e. the accuracy of the results provided.

We shall now demonstrate how such test data can be used to ensure the validity of the 'contractor's' model and verify the effectiveness of its code.

Use of unexpected data

The 'contractor's' model incorporates five input parameters:

- The length of the building
- The width of the building
- The height of the building
- The number of windows
- The number of doors

In developing a formal model, the modeller must ensure that the model user *cannot* input rogue data. For example, the height, width and length of the building should be non-negative numbers. Also, the number of windows and doors must be integers in addition to being non-negative. A model to be used by an end user with limited spreadsheet experience should be supported by ample instructions in the form of a comprehensive user guide (this will be described in the next chapter). Additionally, there should be adequate prompts provided by the model in response to rogue data entry. Figure 5.16 in the previous chapter illustrated the automated routine incorporated in the 'contractor's' model which deals with the entry of the model's parameters.

Although the code used in this routine is specific to Microsoft Excel, it is conceptually simple and most spreadsheet users will be able to understand its purpose. Users of other spreadsheets should be aware that equivalent facilities may be available in the software they regularly use. The benefit of including this routine will be measured by the reader becoming aware of the capabilities of the software in ensuring that data entered in a formal model is valid. Moreover, a detailed description of how to construct an automated routine using specialist macro words was addressed in Chapter 5.

When activating the input data macro, a dialog box appears on the screen, in which the end user types the dimensions of the building, i.e. its length, height and width, plus the number of windows and doors. When constructing a dialog box, the modeller can specify the first three parameters to be *numbers* and the last two to be *integers*. This ensures that any rogue data entry, such as $1\frac{1}{2}$ doors or the text 'DOG' for the building's length, will result in the parameters not being accepted by the model.

Additionally the section of code:

$$= \text{WHILE(OR(length} < 0, \text{height} < 0, \text{width} < 0, \text{windows,}) < 0, \text{doors} < 0))$$
$$= \text{DIALOG.BOX(input\_screen)}$$

is used to ensure that the input parameters are not accepted if any one of them is negative in value. As a consequence, the modeller has developed an input routine which is not only user-friendly in appearance (as shown by the dialog box presented in Chapter 5) but is also robust when faced with rogue data. In short, the whole routine ensures that the 'contractor's' model can respond appropriately to unexpected or inappropriate data entry.

Moreover, it is good practice for the modeller to develop a data set to test the model's input routine. An appropriate data set is illustrated in Figure 6.3.

The aim of this data set is to ensure that the model's input routine can respond in the appropriate way when text is entered instead of numbers, when real numbers are entered instead of integers and when negative numbers are entered instead of positive ones. The table shows the expected model response for each data value. The data set can be used during the testing of the input routine and the modeller can be satisfied that the routine is working properly if the responses of the model agree with those listed in Figure 6.3.

Variable	Data set 1	Data set 2	Data set 3	Data set 4
LENGTH	26	15	20	15
WIDTH	10	CAT	10	10
HEIGHT	−6	10	12	10
WINDOWS	2	1	$2\frac{1}{4}$	2
DOORS	1	1	2	2
RESULT	Not accepted (Height)	Not accepted (Width)	Not accepted (Windows)	Accepted

Figure 6.3 Data set for testing the model's input routine

Use of simple data

Simple data can be used to ensure that each formula in the model functions correctly. In the 'contractor's' model, this can be used to verify the code relating to the formulae for:

- Calculating the area of the building to be decorated
- Calculating time from area using the simple regression equation
- The evaluation of whether a particular prediction of time represents interpolation or extrapolation
- The computation of contract cost from the predicted duration

Because the model under consideration is simple, comparison with the results provided by an electronic calculator will be straightforward.

Consider the simple data set below:

LENGTH OF BUILDING	10
WIDTH OF BUILDING	10
HEIGHT OF BUILDING	10
NO. OF DOORS	1
NO. OF WINDOWS	1

These numbers are simple values which permit the validation of the model's equation to be undertaken quickly and accurately.

Using the formula to calculate area, i.e:

$$AREA = 2*HEIGHT*(LENGTH+WIDTH)-((DOOR*21)+(WINDOW*15))$$
$$= 2*10*(10+10)-(21+15)$$
$$= 364 \text{ square feet}$$

From the regression output:

$$TIME = -1.004+0.048*AREA$$
$$= -1.004+(0.048*364)$$
$$= 18.476 \text{ hours}$$

From the data used to develop the model, the range of contract sizes (area) used was between 200 and 450 square feet. For the test data, the calculated area of 364 square feet lies within this range, and, therefore, the prediction of contract duration represents 'INTERPOLATION'.

Finally, for a contract of 18.476 hours duration, the hourly rate is £11.50. Therefore, the contract cost is:

$$COST = 11.50*18.476$$
$$= £212.47$$

Thus, for the simple data used:

$$AREA = 364$$
$$TIME = 18.476$$
$$PREDICTION = INTERPOLATION$$
$$COST = £212.47$$

The modeller can compare these values with those produced by the spreadsheet model. If the results are the same, the modeller can be satisfied that the code present on the spreadsheet is correct.

Moreover, if range or cell names have been utilized in the creation of the model's code, then the verification process can be much simplified. For example, the mathematical formula:

$$= 2*HEIGHT*(LENGTH+WIDTH)-((DOOR*21)+(WINDOW*15))$$

is much easier to understand than:

$$= 2*W47*(W43+W45)-((W51*21)+(W49*15))$$

Use of normal data

Normal data may be collected from the contracts used to test the model at the prototype stage. This data should be representative of the contracts whose duration and costs will be calculated by the spreadsheet model. Moreover, the level of accuracy offered by the model can be determined and used as a measure of the model's validity. This test will indicate whether additional data and subsequent programming are required.

Finally, once the three sets of data have been collected, they can be utilized in any additional validation and verification of the model.

ADVANTAGES OF THE BLOCK STRUCTURE

The underpinning assumption in this book is that the modeller has utilized a block structure in the development of a formal spreadsheet model. Figure 6.4 provides a subset of such a structure, incorporating the input, process (model), results and named range blocks.

In practice, it is the contents of the four blocks listed which will be scrutinized during the validation and verification process. Moreover, if the areas of input, process (i.e. the 'model' itself) and output remain separate, then the validation and verification process can be greatly simplified. In particular, the input routine described earlier is easy to follow and test because all of the parameters used are housed within one self-contained block of the model, i.e. on the input screen. Additionally, the model code which must be verified using simple test data is located totally within the output block. Therefore, in both cases, the required code is easy to locate and

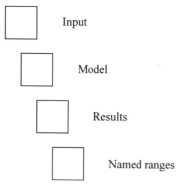

Figure 6.4 A spreadsheet map as a self-contained block of a model

subsequently test. Moreover, because the formulae utilize *range or cell names* as suggested in Chapter 4, then the verification process is greatly simplified.

AUDITING A SPREADSHEET MODEL

In order to verify a complex spreadsheet model, it may be necessary for the modeller to audit each formula constructed within the model. A number of modern spreadsheets offer auditing facilities which can be used to facilitate this part of the verification process. Microsoft Excel offers a useful function which performs three important roles:

- It displays the formula present in the cell under consideration
- It identifies all the formulae (or cells) present in the model which are dependent upon a particular cell. These cells are called *dependents*
- It shows all formulae (or cells) in the spreadsheet on which the particular cell is dependent. These cells are referred to as *precedents*

In order to determine this information for a particular cell, the modeller must highlight the relevant cell and select:

Options

Workspace

and click on **Info Window** in the Display menu.

By clicking on **Info** on the menu, the required information can be added to this window for the chosen cell or formula. At a maximum, the resultant window which appears on the screen will house the following information:

Cell
Formula
Value
Format
Protect
Names
Precedents
Dependents
Notes

By inspecting the information shown in this window (in particular the precedents and dependents), the modeller can verify the accuracy of the formula by comparing it with the conceptual model used to develop the spreadsheet application under construction. Figure 6.5 shows the information corresponding to the cell containing the estimate of TIME in the 'contractor's' model.

In particular, one potential problem which may be rectified by using this Excel facility is the circular reference. Such a reference can prove problematic to the modeller when writing formulae for a spreadsheet model, and occurs when a cell resident in the spreadsheet refers to itself either directly or indirectly. For example, if the cell D100 contains the formula =**AVERAGE(D90:D100)** then the circular reference is direct. In contrast, if cell E50 contains the formula +**E52/2** and cell E52 contains the formula +**E50** the reference is indirect. If such a reference is made, Excel will display the message '**Cannot Solve Circular References**'. By displaying formula, dependents and precedents information for each cell in the model, this type of reference can be easily corrected. Additionally, one of the affected formulae will be referenced

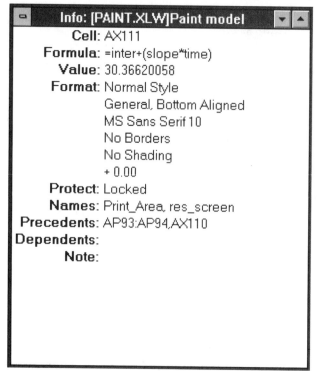

Figure 6.5   Cell information provided by Excel

on the spreadsheet's status bar, e.g. **Circular Reference:A4**. On the relatively rare occasions when circular references are appropriate, these will be indicated by the conceptual model constructed prior to spreadsheet development.

Finally, if a list of named ranges is produced, this process of formulae verification is much simplified and the advantages of having a list of live cells and ranges of cells should be apparent.

ACCURACY AND PRESENTATION OF RESULTS

Chapter 4 described an effective method of constructing and presenting complex calculations and formulae in order to facilitate end-user understanding. The validation and verification of a model presents two further issues with regard to presentation and understanding of spreadsheet formulae:

- The accuracy of the input data
- The accuracy and presentation of the results

The input data used to quantify the relationships in a spreadsheet model may well have been subject to approximation or rounding. Quite often, this simplification will not have been performed by the modeller. Moreover, the modeller might not even be aware it has taken place. As a consequence, the level of accuracy must be recognized by the modeller before constructing the code which deals with the model's output. For example, if the duration of contracts in the 'contractor's' model is measured to the nearest hour, then any prediction made by the model for the duration of a future contract should not be presented to a greater level of accuracy.

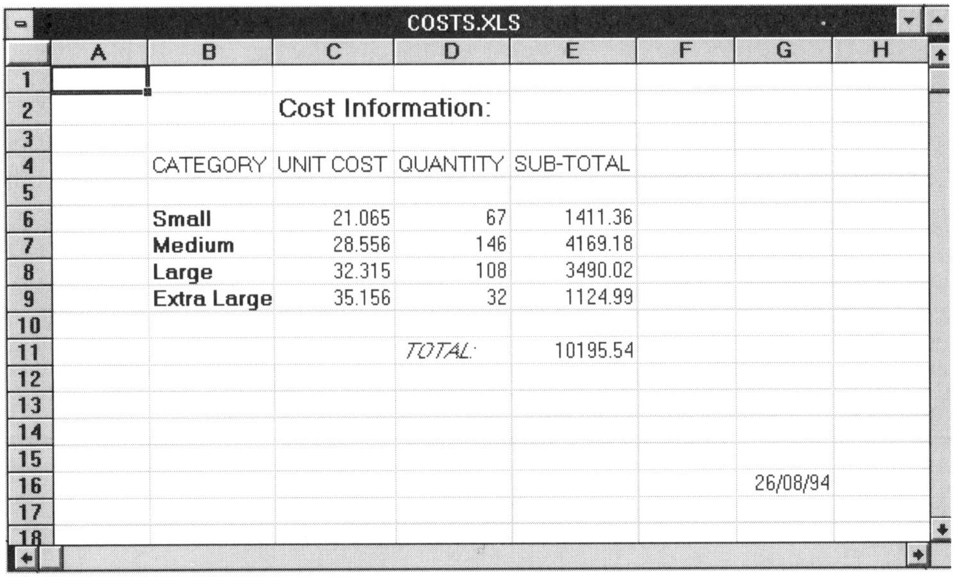

Figure 6.6   Spreadsheet output displaying misleading results

A major feature of most spreadsheets is that its internal accuracy is at least as great as the actual values displayed. This internal accuracy may lead to the presentation of some misleading results. Consider the simple cost data presented in Figure 6.6.

The sum of the four values in column E illustrates the problems which may be caused by formatting a range of cells. The total value for each category, i.e. the range of cells E6:E9, has been formatted to two decimal places. The total cost resident in cell E11 has also been formatted in the same way. Anybody utilizing this cost data may find the results misleading because the sum of 1411.36, 4169.18, 3490.02 and 1124.99 is equal to 10 195.55 *not* 10 195.54. The problems of rounding and significant figures can be overcome by utilizing certain functions available in the spreadsheet. For example, Microsoft Excel offers the **=ROUND( )** and **=INT( )** facilities which may help prevent such spurious results being produced. In practice, the level of accuracy required in the presentation of results will vary between modelling applications.

CONCLUSIONS

This chapter has described the process of model validation and verification. Verification examines the logic of the spreadsheet code and is the process which ensures that the formulae incorporated into the model are consistent with the relationships identified in the conceptual model. Validity is the process which examines the accuracy of the model's output. Moreover, once a model is identified as being invalid, the modelling process becomes iterative, especially with respect to problem conceptualization and model testing.

Additionally, the process can be facilitated by producing appropriate test data. This test data falls into three categories:

- Extreme or unexpected data to test the model's input routine
- Simple data to test the model's formulae
- Normal data to test the overall validity and performance of the model

Testing of a formal model can be made more efficient if the areas of input, process and output remain separate. This efficiency can be made possible if the modeller has utilized a block layout similar to those described in Chapter 3.

Finally, the necessity for suitable presentation of results and awareness of the accuracy of input data has been addressed within the framework of the validation and verification process. The need to eliminate results from a formal model which are spurious in appearance should be apparent.

REVIEW QUESTIONS

1. Define the term 'validation' using words and diagrams.
2. Define the term 'verification'.
3. Explain why the process of validation and verification illustrates the iterative nature of the (spreadsheet) modelling process.
4. Describe in detail the three different types of test data required to ensure the validity of, and verify the logic of, a formal spreadsheet model.
5. Why is it useful at this stage of the modelling process to use range or cell names in spreadsheet formulae?
6. Using a spreadsheet with which you are familiar, construct an input routine for the dimensions of a building, which ensure that:
   – The height is at least 10 feet
   – The length is at least 12 feet
   – The width is at least 8 feet
   Moreover, ensure that the number of doors and windows input are non-negative and less than three. Assume that the respective standard sizes of doors and windows are 12 and 18 square feet. Additionally, ensure that your routines can reject variables input as text and the total area of the building is non-negative.
7. For the problem described in Question 6, develop a suitable set of test data for each of the model's parameters.
8. What two factors should be considered when validating the output of a spreadsheet model?
9. Why should the accuracy of input data be of importance to the modeller?
10. What is meant by the term 'circular reference'?
11. Describe the main features of a spreadsheet's auditing facility.
12. Name two functions which can prevent the output from a spreadsheet model appearing spurious. What causes this spurious appearance?

CASE STUDY QUESTIONS

1. If an auditing facility exists in your spreadsheet, produce the following:
   – A list of all formulae in the model which are dependent upon a particular cell (i.e. especially those cells which correspond to the model's input parameters)
   – A list of all formulae present in the model
   – Identify any circular references. If any exist, check your code with the conceptual model and alter the incorrect code (in this model no circular references should exist)
   If no auditing facility exists, undertake the steps listed above manually.
2. Compare the list of formulae and dependent relationships identified from the spreadsheet model with the influence diagram prepared earlier. Ensure that the logic of the spreadsheet code is consistent with the conceptual model.

3. Prepare a set of simple test data and determine whether the calculations housed in the spreadsheet model are correct, i.e the calculation of NPV is accurate. Remember to check the assumptions implicit in any built-in functions offered by the spreadsheet.

4. If any investment calculations have been undertaken manually, compare the results of the manual calculations (i.e. using the everyday data) with the output produced by the spreadsheet model.

5. Create a data set containing extreme values (i.e. text instead of numbers, negative values, non-integer values, etc.) and check that the model's input routine is working properly, i.e. it can reject rogue input data. The input variables which need to be considered are:
    - Unit sales in the first year
    - Growth rate per annum (%)
    - Price per unit (£)
    - Cost per unit (£)
    - Interest rate (%)
    - Amount invested (£)

6. Examine the calculations housed in the model. Ensure that any rounding of values to enhance model presentation has not resulted in the model's output having a misleading appearance.

SEVEN

MODEL DOCUMENTATION

OVERVIEW

This chapter describes the need for comprehensive documentation to support the effective application of a structured spreadsheet model by an end user. The concept of spreadsheet mapping is considered again, and, in turn, it is shown how a spreadsheet map can be used to underpin the different types of documentation that should accompany a structured model. The ideas of internal (spreadsheet) documentation, external (technical) documentation and the provision of a comprehensive user-guide will be discussed.

OBJECTIVES

After reading this chapter and working through the questions, the reader will be able to:

- Understand why it is necessary to provide comprehensive documentation to support a structured spreadsheet model.
- Construct a spreadsheet map using a combination of cell references and diagrams.
- Demonstrate how this map can be used to underpin a model's documentation.
- Differentiate between the different types of documentation required to support a formal model.
- Identify the different users of the various types of model documentation.

INTRODUCTION

So far, this book has described how a spreadsheet can afford a modeller powerful numerical and programming facilities within an informal and flexible computing environment. In turn, these features can be incorporated within a formal model structure and the resultant model can be used as an effective decision-making tool. As a consequence, many business modellers have developed formal, spreadsheet models to support effective decision-making. Additionally, the idea of constructing business models for 'one-off' solutions has been replaced by descriptive models, which in turn are often used by a third party. Many of these end users have limited experience of computers, and, as a consequence, the documentation and presentation of the spreadsheet model is of considerable importance.

Moreover, many spreadsheet modellers are primarily business modellers and secondly programmers. A number of these modellers have perhaps not understood that the models they develop require comprehensive documentation.

Some modellers may consider that rigorous documentation criteria infringe on the informal environment that the spreadsheet provides. Additionally, many modellers believe the spreadsheet to be self-documenting. Both these suggestions are untrue. In comparison to high-level programming languages such as Fortran or Pascal, which employ mathematical statements and quasi-English code, the code can be particularly difficult for an end user with limited spreadsheet knowledge to interpret and it is fair to say that this code is infamous for being poorly documented.

The aim of this chapter is to describe the appropriate documentation which should accompany a formal (spreadsheet) model. The documentation required to support the application and maintenance of such a model by an end user is classified into three groups in this chapter:

- A guide for the model's user
- Internal (spreadsheet) documentation
- External (technical) documentation

Additionally, these areas of documentation should be underpinned by the development of a comprehensive spreadsheet map. The examples and illustrations provided in the chapter are based on the simple 'contractor's' model developed using Microsoft Excel.

THE SPREADSHEET MAP

Arguably, the most important feature in a model's documentation is the spreadsheet map. This map can be either a diagrammatical representation of, or a set of references to, the model's layout. Additionally, it may be useful in a number of situations to combine both the diagrammatical map and the cell references. Initially any formal model should be drafted on paper prior to any spreadsheet development. This blueprint should take into account the volume of data input, the subsequent processing of the data and the output to be provided by the model. Mapping the model's contents can also ensure that these areas remain separate in the model by utilizing a block structure layout as described in Chapter 3.

Moreover, any modification to the developing model should be initially mapped (on paper) before spreadsheet development is undertaken. The advantage of constructing a map is that the modeller will not only be aware of the location of each self-contained section in the model, but also the location of the contents within these separate blocks. In particular, adopting both a block structure and undertaking mapping will help prevent an overlap between the 'functional' areas of input, process and output. The help screen for the 'contractor's' model was shown in Figure 4.2, and is reproduced here as Figure 7.1 for convenience. This model has adopted the block structure, with the first block (the introduction screen) being located in cells A1:I17. In this particular model, the modeller will have decided the contents of the help screen prior to any spreadsheet development.

Since the ('contractor's') model is small and the code is relatively non-complex, the menu instructions and top-level mapping details are perfectly adequate for an end user with limited experience of spreadsheets. For more complex models, the help facility may need to be more supportive and perhaps extend to more than one screen. Effective mapping will facilitate a suitable layout.

The areas of importance on the help screen shown in Figure 7.1 are the (screen) title, menu instructions and top-level navigational details. Figure 7.2 illustrates a subset of the model's map

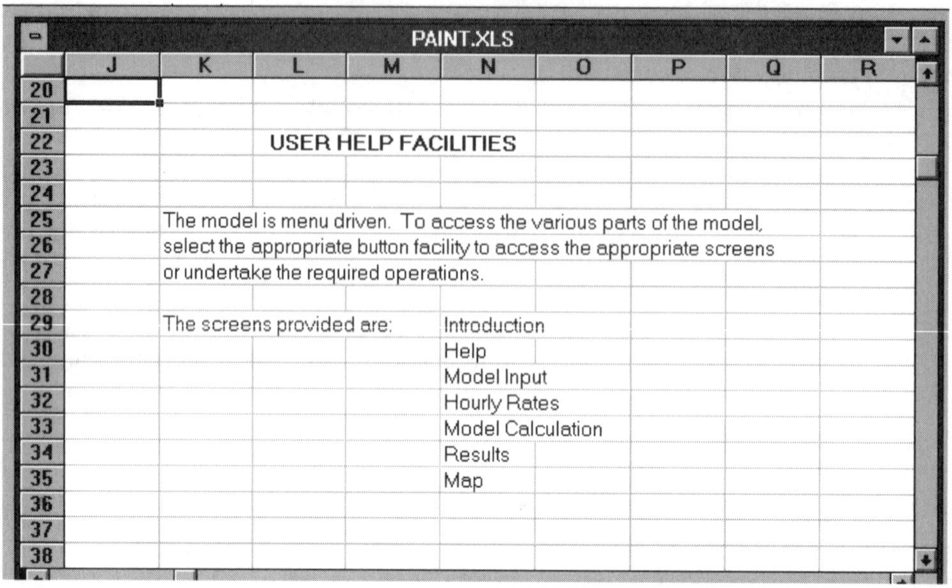

Figure 7.1 Help screen for a spreadsheet model

which corresponds to this help screen. This map is simply a set of cell references corresponding to the various parts of the model.

The type of map considered in Figure 7.2 can be formulated using a 'top-down' approach in which the main sections of the model are listed first (e.g. introduction screen, help screen, etc.) followed by groups of 'sub-ranges' in descending order of location. Alternatively, the set of named ranges may be listed alphabetically (with one column containing the names and an adjacent one housing the ranges). An alphabetic list can be generated in Microsoft Excel activating:

Formula
Paste Name followed by **Paste List**

Moreover, the spreadsheet map itself can be allocated a self-contained block within the model, perhaps adjacent to the help screens, as shown in Figure 7.3. This map can then be accessed (by hand or by navigational macro) and scrutinized by the model user. Alternatively, if the model is small, the whole map can be located on the introductory screen. The diagrammatical layout pictured in Figure 7.3 can also be used as a top-level on-screen map by adding cell references to each separate block.

Introductory screen	A1:I17
User help screen	J20:R38
Screen reference	L27:O33
Navigational details	L27:O33

Figure 7.2 Subset of a spreadsheet map

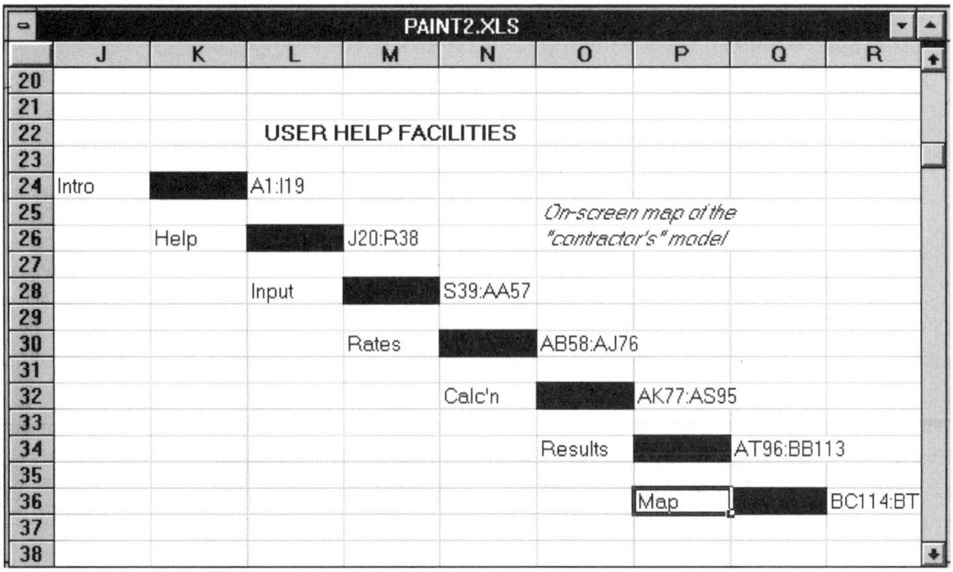

Figure 7.3   A spreadsheet map as a self-contained block of a model

Additionally, the introduction or help screen of a larger model may include 'top-level' mapping details corresponding to the main areas of the model. This is illustrated on the help screen displayed in Figure 7.4, where the locations of the main areas of the model are provided in cells at the bottom of the screen.

The main advantage of developing a spreadsheet map is that structure is given initially to the model and secondly to its supporting documentation. Without either (model) structure or adequate documentation, a potentially effective spreadsheet model may become little more

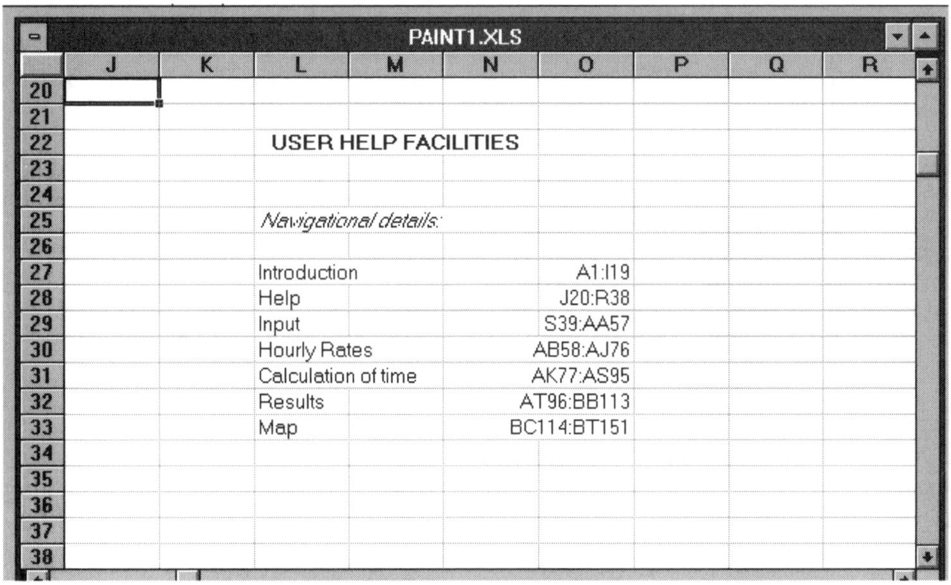

Figure 7.4   Top-level navigational details

than a block of cells. Once a spreadsheet map has been developed, the three areas of documentation listed in the introduction to this chapter can be produced.

Moreover, the more sophisticated spreadsheets (Excel included) provide a number of built-in commands which facilitate the construction of a detailed, technical map. These features are discussed fully in the section of this chapter which considers the external (or technical) documentation.

A GUIDE FOR THE MODEL'S USER

If a formal spreadsheet model has been developed, it is likely that the end user may have only limited computing experience. In many cases, the amount of time spent by the end user using a PC may be too insignificant to warrant formal spreadsheet training. In response to such an audience, the modeller should always provide a comprehensive user-guide. This guide should not use spreadsheet terminology, but non-technical English. In writing a user-guide to support *any* formal spreadsheet model, the modeller should perhaps always 'play safe' and assume that the end user has little or no knowledge of spreadsheet operations.

The detail required in the user-guide will be dictated by the size and intricacy of the model developed. Additionally, the needs and expertise of the model user should also influence the guide's *content and style*. However skilled this model user may be, the guide should not be just a hard copy of the model's internal documentation. Instead the modeller should ensure that it is both a practical and comprehensive (non-technical) supplement.

A user-guide should include the following features:

1. *A description in business terms of the role of the spreadsheet model.* This should include any assumptions made and highlight any limitations in the results provided. In particular, this description should discuss the source of data within the organization, formulae used in the model and how the output is used to facilitate decision-making. A suitable description for the 'contractor's' model is given below.

   The model considers the dimensions of a building which needs to be painted. The dimensions required are the building's length, width and height measured in feet. Additionally, the number of doors and windows must be recorded. Using this information, the area of the building can be calculated using the formula:

   $$AREA = 2*HEIGHT*(LENGTH+WIDTH)-((21*DOORS)+(15*WINDOWS))$$

   In this formula, an assumption has been made that all doors and windows are of a standard size, namely 21 and 15 square feet respectively.

   Once the area of a building has been calculated, contract time is estimated using the simple regression equation:

   $$TIME = -1.004 + 0.048 \times AREA$$

   Implicit in using this formula are the assumptions that the experience of individual workmen and the condition of the building do not affect contract time. The data used to determine the relationship between time and area was collected from ten contracts recently completed by the company.

   Once time has been calculated, contract cost can be determined using the formula:

   $$COST = HOURLY\ RATE*TIME$$

The hourly rate used in this formula also depends on the estimate duration of the contract. A set of hourly rates is stored within the model.

In general, some of the formulae used in a formal model may be industrial standards. If so, then reference should made to their derivation.

2. *A fully detailed spreadsheet map.* As described earlier, the map can facilitate both end-user understanding of the model and navigation to its separate sections. For an end user with limited spreadsheet experience, a map similar to that illustrated in Figure 7.3, incorporating cell references, may be particularly useful.

3. *Instructions on model access.* For an Excel user, the instructions may read:

Double-click on the Microsoft Excel icon and on entering the spreadsheet select:

<u>F</u>ile
<u>O</u>pen

On accessing Excel, the window will resemble Figure 7.5.

In such a situation, the guide should instruct the model user to:

> Select **a**: from the list of drives
> Highlight the filename **PAINT.XLW**
> Click on **OK**
> To access the model, select **Model** from the workbook.

Additionally, there should be instructions, if necessary, on how the end user should save the updated model. This will be discussed for the 'contractor's' model in part 5 of the user guide.

4. *Details of the form in which the data should be input.* For example, in the 'contractor's' model, the dimensions of the building are the input requirements for the model. In response, the user-guide should indicate the units of measurement, i.e. feet. In general, the level of accuracy of the data should be discussed. For example, a company cashflow model may involve values of cash in the order of millions of pounds. Any supporting user-guide should indicate whether the model requires exact cash values or whether they are to be input, say, to the nearest thousand pounds. Additionally, details on data collection within the

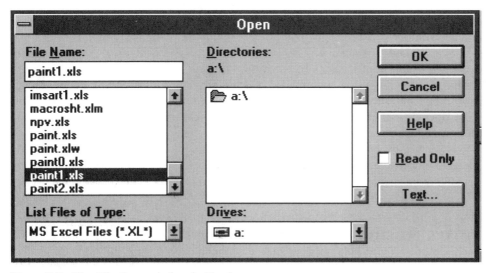

Figure 7.5 The File Open window in Excel

organization should be mentioned, especially if it is not obvious to the model user. This was indicated for the simple 'contractor's' model in the business description.

5. *Perhaps of greatest importance*: list precise instructions on how to use the model.   For the 'contractor's' model these steps would consist of the following.

On loading the model **PAINT.XLW** a set of macro buttons will appear on the screen. To view any individual part of the model, select the appropriate macro button, e.g. clicking on **Results** allows the model user to view the model's output screen. To calculate the time and cost for a new contract, the dimensions of the building must be entered. To enter the new data, select

Input

from the set of buttons displayed on the introductory screen of the model. The input screen will appear in addition to two further macro buttons:

Input data   Intro screen

By selecting **Input data**, a dialog box will appear on the spreadsheet screen. Once the data has been entered select **Intro screen** to leave the input area of the model.

To obtain the contract time and cost, click on the **Results** button. The results screen will appear in addition to two further macro buttons:

Print   Intro screen

After viewing/printing the results, select **Intro screen**. If the model needs to be saved select:

Save

Finally, to exit the model, select

Quit

6. *A comprehensive description of all model automation.*   This description should incorporate details of individual macros, their purpose and how they are invoked. A line-by-line description of the individual macro code may be useful, especially when the code is complex. If appropriate, details of any macro menus or macro buttons (as used in the 'contractor's' model) should also be included. For an end user with limited spreadsheet experience, a systematic description of selecting the menu options may be particularly useful.

7. *Complete, unambiguous instructions if the model user is required to use basic spreadsheet commands.*   An example of basic commands may include changing the print options for an individual printer or saving an updated model. Obviously, the complex spreadsheet operations should be automated, especially for a model user with little or no training in spreadsheet operations. As stressed throughout this book, the 'contractor's' model was written for an end user with no spreadsheet training.

8. *Diagrams, in particular screen print-outs and Excel windows wherever appropriate.*   This should help to increase user understanding of both the model and accompanying user guide. These diagrams should be similar to those used and referred to throughout this book.

INTERNAL (SPREADSHEET) DOCUMENTATION

Programmers using high-level languages have long understood the need for program documentation. The internal documentation in such programs takes the form of comments written between sections of code. Many programmers consider it useful to include descriptive information within a program. In particular, such comments, which are written inside braces { } in Pascal for example, are helpful in that they clarify the meaning of individual statements whose aims may be unclear, and they can be used to define the purpose of individual blocks of code.

In the same way, a formal spreadsheet model should be suitably documented. This internal documentation needs to serve two occasionally overlapping roles, namely:

- To facilitate end user understanding
- To assist those with the responsibility of maintaining the model

Internal documentation for the end user

Any model developed for an end user with limited spreadsheet knowledge should always contain a detailed introductory screen. From a user's perspective, this is arguably the most important part of the model's internal documentation. The essential details that could be included in the introductory screen are:

- A meaningful title
- A non-technical description
- Details of technical aid
- Navigation details or, if appropriate, mapping details where the level of detail is determined by the size and complexity of the model

Figure 7.6 illustrates a suitable introductory screen for a formal model, incorporating most of the features listed above.

In contrast, the introductory screen illustrated in Figure 7.7 (the 'contractor's' model) does not contain any navigational details. Instead, this model incorporates macro buttons which,

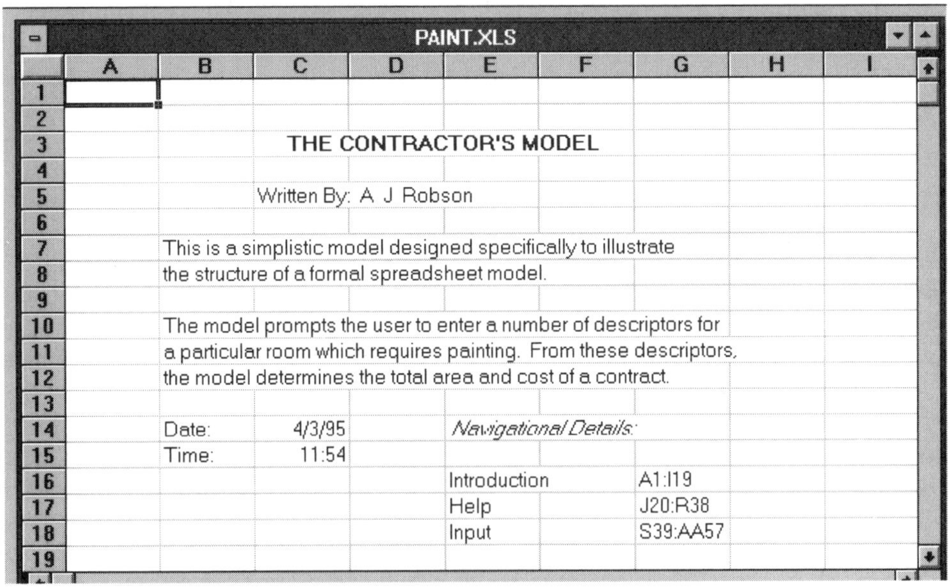

Figure 7.6 An introductory screen for a formal spreadsheet model

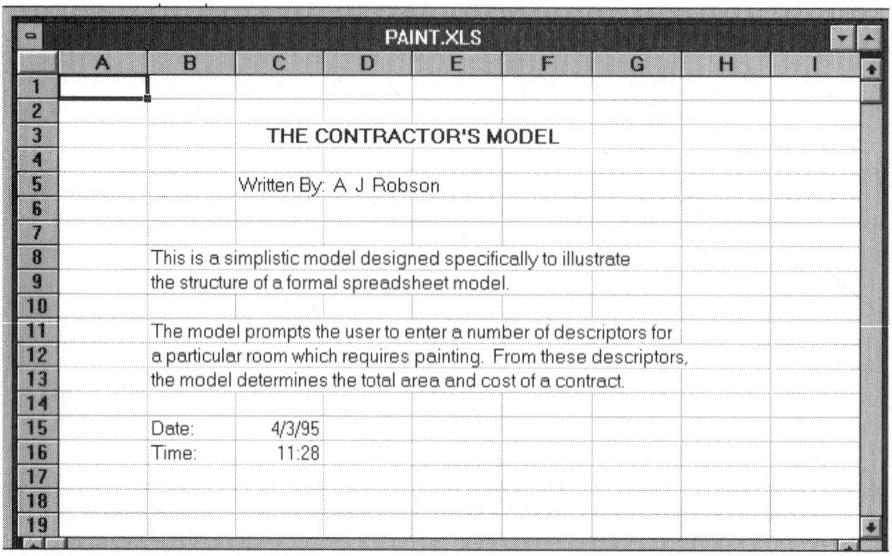

Figure 7.7   An introductory screen without mapping details

on activation, facilitate efficient user navigation. In smaller spreadsheet models, the introductory page may, if appropriate, contain details on macro execution, like that screen pictured in Figure 7.4. For larger models, it is better to locate this documentation on (adjacent) help screens.

Moreover, each screen on the spreadsheet which can be accessed by the model user should be appropriately documented. In most cases, a number of lines of text will be sufficient. Many spreadsheets offer word-processing facilities, which can be utilized to produce this documentation. As described earlier, a spreadsheet map may be incorporated into the model's internal documentation. The level of detail provided should be tailored to suit the needs of the end user.

Internal documentation for model maintenance

In many situations, a business process may undergo a number of significant changes. In response to such changes, a spreadsheet model may have to be updated. To facilitate such maintenance, it is important to invest time in the initial development of the model's internal documentation. This part of the internal documentation covers three main areas: the documentation of formulae, named ranges and macro automation.

It is important to document all formulae used in the model. This can be achieved by writing the formulae as text (perhaps adjacent to the live cell containing the actual formula) and defining each variable and constant used. Where a formula has been copied, it is usually only necessary to document the cell containing the original formula.

Like the model user-guide, range names used in the model should be listed on-screen and their contents documented. In the 'contractor's' model, the range names were located on their own separate screen.

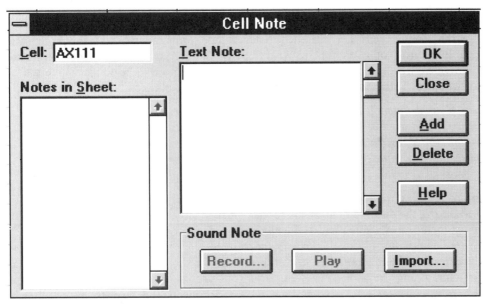

Figure 7.8 Excel's Formula Note window

One additional and very useful Excel facility is the provision for adding notes to each formula used in the model. This can be achieved by highlighting the cell housing the formula and selecting:

Formula
Note

and typing the appropriate note in the **Text Note** window. This window is shown in Figure 7.8. Typically, on-screen notes may include formula derivation and, where necessary, reference to appropriate texts and business reports or projects.

If an output screen contains formulae and is likely to be printed by the model user, it may be more appropriate to locate the on-screen documentation on adjacent screens which will not be printed.

Finally, a short description of all macros and their function should be given, while detailed comments should be included with the macro code on the macro sheet that accompanies the formal model. It is useful to use two columns in the presentation of a macro, the first column containing the macro code and the second a line-by-line explanation. For more complicated macros, it will prove useful to provide each line with an individual explanation. Macro documentation has been covered in greater detail in Chapter 5.

EXTERNAL (TECHNICAL) DOCUMENTATION

The spreadsheet model's external documentation is written for those who will monitor the performance of, and, where necessary, update, the model. Consequently, the external documentation is a technical reference, and therefore must be written in spreadsheet terminology. A number of features must be included in the model's external documentation. Arguably the most important feature is a description of the background to the model's development and its role within the organization's decision-making process.

In general, the external documentation should contain the following features:

1. Primarily, the *terms of reference* should be listed. These terms indicate why the model was developed. The terms of reference are written prior to the model's development and are usually provided by the end user. For the 'contractor's' model, the following terms of reference would be sufficient:

   Develop a simplistic model designed specifically to determine the cost of painting a building of a specific area. The model should prompt the model user to enter a number of descriptors for a particular building which requires painting. From these descriptors, the model should determine the total area of the building and then the contract duration and cost. Doors and windows can be assumed to be of a standard size.

   For more complex applications of the spreadsheet, it is likely that these terms will have to be revised during the development of the model. In such situations, the technical documentation must include any subsequent refinements and, if appropriate, discussion about their inclusion.

2. Since the external documentation is written primarily for those modellers who are responsible for maintaining the model, it is important to provide a *technical description*. This discusses in spreadsheet terminology how the model meets the business requirements. Such a description should refer to the formulae or built-in functions utilized in the model, and it may be useful to provide background information about such formulae, including reference to textbooks or legal considerations. Moreover, any external sources used to derive the formulae included in the model should be discussed. If the modeller has made any assumptions or simplifications during the development of the model, the technical description should contain these details. For example, in the 'contractor's' model, the technical description should describe:

   - The use of the built-in regression facility to determine contract time from building size, i.e. the built-in **INTERCEPT( )** and **SLOPE( )** functions, where the x data represented building area and the y data contract time.
   - The source of information used in the regression model to determine contract time by area, i.e. the size and duration of ten contracts recently completed by the company.
   - The derivation of the formula for the building's size, including the assumption of constant-sized doors and windows, and references to the constant sizes used.

     In this model, assume that each contract undertaken will involve buildings of a simple rectangular structure, comprising two long walls and two short walls. In practice, there may be contracts which involve decorating buildings of irregular shape. However, by assuming that each building has a simple structure, the formulae considered in the resultant model will be easier to understand.

     Assume that the long wall is of height H (feet) and length L, while the shorter wall is of height H and width W (refer to Figure 2.1). Assuming a simple four-wall building:

$$\text{Area of the 'long' wall} = \text{LENGTH*HEIGHT}$$
$$\text{Area of the 'short' wall} = \text{WIDTH*HEIGHT}$$
$$\text{Total area} = 2*(\text{LENGTH*HEIGHT} + \text{WIDTH*HEIGHT})$$
$$= 2*\text{HEIGHT}*(\text{LENGTH} + \text{WIDTH})$$

If the standard area of the doors and windows is 21 and 15 square feet respectively, then:

$$\text{Total area of the doors in the building} = 21*\text{DOORS}$$
$$\text{Total area of the windows} = 15*\text{WINDOWS}$$

Therefore, the required formula for the area to be painted is:

2*HEIGHT*(LENGTH+WIDTH)–((21*DOORS)+(15*WINDOWS))

– The source of the cost information housed in the model's 'lookup' table. That is, the company offers a discount rate depending upon the size of contract being undertaken. Currently the hourly rates are:

Contract duration (hours)	Hourly rate (£)
0–	12.75
10–	11.50
20–	10.85
30–	9.75
40–	9.50
50–	9.00
100–	8.00

Obviously, as a model increases in complexity, this technical description becomes more detailed.

3. Like the other documentation described, this technical reference should also include a detailed *spreadsheet map*. A high-level map, presented in the block structure with block cell references (as pictured in Figure 7.3), may be a useful inclusion. A number of spreadsheets, Excel included, incorporate customized 'auditing facilities' which can be used to facilitate the development of a detailed, technical map. The main use of an auditing facility is analysing the formulae present in a model, displaying formulae information, identifying formulae depending on the contents of certain cells and those which are involved in circular reference. Such output provides a technical detailed map indicating the contents and nature of each live cell. Additionally, by highlighting (in turn) each *live cell/formula* used in the model and invoking the Excel command:

Options
Workspace

followed by clicking on **Info Window** in the Display menu, the required information can be generated and this may be used as part of the external documentation.

Figure 7.9 illustrates the information sheet for the TIME formula used in the 'contractor's' model. Moreover, if the modeller has used range names in the formulae (as shown for the formula under consideration), the information provided in this sheet (in particular precedents, dependents, names and formulae) will become more meaningful and, as a result, will be easy to read and understand.

4. Like the internal documentation, this technical reference should contain *a list of all named ranges* in the model. Moreover, after this table has been generated it may be useful to differentiate between input, process and output ranges in the technical guide.

5. This technical reference must include a detailed, technical description of all *macros* used in the model. For the more complicated macros, any additional comments made about each line in the macro routine will prove invaluable.

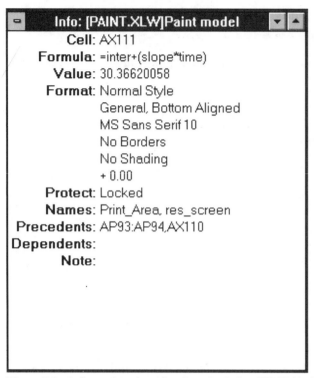

Figure 7.9   Information sheet for the calculation TIME in the 'contractor's' model

6. Finally, if data and model security are important, the modeller may have utilized the pass-
    word features provided by Excel. If these facilities have been used, the technical guide (in
    particular *only* the technical guide) should detail the type of password protection used. Using
    password and model security is described later in Chapter 9 as an additional topic.

    As described for the model user guide, the presentation and quality of the external guide can
be enhanced by the inclusion of screen print-outs and spreadsheet windows.

CONCLUSIONS

This chapter has described the appropriate documentation that should accompany a structured,
formal (spreadsheet) model. Three types of essential documentation have been outlined, necessary in supporting the use and maintenance of such a model by an end user and modelling
personnel.

    Specifically, the three areas of model documentation should be underpinned by the develop-
ment of a comprehensive spreadsheet map. This map may be a diagrammatical representation of
the model, a list of cell and range references or a combination of both diagram and cell references.
Additionally, the chapter has described the development of this map and suggested how its
differing role and appearance can be incorporated within the three types of documentation.

    This chapter has assumed that the documentation produced has a dual role, namely to
facilitate end-user understanding and also to assist those with the responsibility of maintaining
and supporting the model.

REVIEW QUESTIONS

1. Explain why a spreadsheet model is not self-documenting, especially in comparison to a high-level programming language.
2. Outline the three types of documentation which are required to support a structured spreadsheet model.
3. Describe and sketch the possible types of spreadsheet map.
4. When should the initial map be created? What are the benefits of producing a map at this stage?
5. Outline the advantages of providing a self-contained block in the model for a spreadsheet map.
6. *Briefly* discuss the advantages of spreadsheet mapping.
7. What factors affect the style and content of a model's user guide? What type of language should be used when writing this guide?
8. List and describe *briefly* the contents of such a guide.
9. Describe *briefly* the two reasons for incorporating documentation on the spreadsheet.
10. From the user's point of view, what is the most important location for spreadsheet documentation? What details should be included?
11. From a maintenance perspective, what areas of the model in particular should be supported?
12. For whom is the technical documentation written? In what style of language should this documentation be written?
13. List and describe *briefly* the essential features of the technical documentation.
14. Describe how a technical map can be developed. What are the advantages of using range names in the model?

CASE STUDY QUESTIONS

1. Produce a detailed spreadsheet map for the investment model.
2. Produce a detailed user-guide suitable for an end user with limited spreadsheet experience. This guide should contain:
   - A description of the role of the model in the decision-making process
   - A detailed spreadsheet map
   - Instructions on model retrieval
   - Details regarding the form in which the data should be input
   - Precise, systematic instructions on how to use the model and interpret its output
   - Any assumptions made during the development of the model
3. Prepare the model's internal documentation. This should include a detailed introduction and help screens, a table of named ranges and a comprehensive on-screen description of all of the formulae contained within the model. If an auditing facility is available, provide a list of all formulae and dependent variables housed in the model. Finally, ensure that all macros are properly documented.
4. Produce a technical guide to support the model's maintenance. In this external documentation, provide terms of reference and a technical description of the model and the calculations used. Additionally, the technical guide should contain details of all formulae used, a set of named ranges and a technical description of all macros and menus.

EIGHT

USING A FORMAL MODEL TO EXPLORE DIFFERENT BUSINESS SCENARIOS

OVERVIEW

This chapter describes the issues which become relevant once a formal spreadsheet model has been developed, accepted and implemented. These issues are concerned with how the spreadsheet allows the model user to explore various business scenarios, and, in order to describe how this may be facilitated, three powerful facilities offered by Excel are considered: the Data Table, the Goal Seek routine and the Scenario Manager.

OBJECTIVES

After reading this chapter and working through the questions, the reader will be able to:

- Recognize how the block structure allows the model user to explore a range of business scenarios.
- Recognize when a data table can be used within a formal spreadsheet model.
- Understand the concept of model optimization and be aware of how the output from the data table may be used to identify the 'best' solution to the problem under consideration.
- Understand how the data table can be used to measure the sensitivity of a model's solution and recognize how its inclusion in a formal model can facilitate 'what if' analysis.
- Understand how a facility called 'goalseek' may be useful in identifying the value of a selected input variable which yields the desired output from a spreadsheet model.
- Understand the term 'scenario' and be able to manage a suite of scenarios using Excel's Scenario Manager facility.

INTRODUCTION

Previous chapters have described the development, testing and documentation of a structured spreadsheet model. In general, the modelling process will not be complete at this stage. Specifically, the model must be accepted by the end user. The degree of success achieved in implementing a particular model will be influenced chiefly by the confidence shown both in its usability (i.e. whether the model is sufficiently user-friendly) and its effectiveness as a decision-making tool. Moreover, there may be occasions when the output produced by the model and resultant decisions made may be resisted within the client organization. Problems encountered during model implementation can be minimized if the modeller and end user are in agreement throughout the development of the model with regard to the assumptions made and the features incorporated.

This chapter will address additional issues which become relevant once the model has been accepted by the end user and is ready to be implemented. These issues are concerned with utilizing facilities offered by the spreadsheet to explore a variety of business scenarios. This experimentation may be either formal or informal in nature, and should be influenced by the complexity of the model and the skills of the model user. End-user experimentation (within a formal modelling environment) will be considered in this chapter by making reference to a simple cashflow model. In considering this particular model, three powerful spreadsheet tools will be described, namely the data table, the goalseek facility and the scenario manager. Arguably the most useful of these facilities is the data table which can be used either to determine the optimal or 'best' solution to the situation being modelled, or as a tool for measuring the sensitivity of a model's output. In the cashflow model to be described in this chapter, a data table is incorporated in order to measure the sensitivity of the model's solution (i.e. end-of-period balance) in response to changes in value of a number of predefined input variables.

BUILDING EFFICIENT SPREADSHEET MODELS

Chapters 2 to 7 have considered the development of a formal spreadsheet model which may be implemented by an end user with limited knowledge of spreadsheet operations. An important feature of the simple model considered is its structure, which ensures that the model's input parameters are located 'outside' its processes and calculations as shown by Figure 8.1.

By adopting this kind of formal model structure, new values for input parameters can be easily entered into the model and their influence can be readily identified by the end user.

In short, if a model has a structure similar to that displayed in Figure 8.1, it is easy to experiment by changing the values of selected input variables (and in turn measure the effect on a model's output). Moreover, by providing navigational macros (as described in Chapter 5), the end user can move efficiently between the separate input and output sections within the formal structure. By doing this, a number of scenarios can be considered both quickly and easily, albeit very informally. In general, such experimentation is known as 'what if' analysis; for example, the end user may wish to ask questions like, '*What* is the effect on end-of-period balance, *if* unit costs increase?'

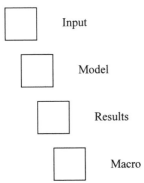

Figure 8.1   A model structure with the input as a separate self-contained section

EXPLORING DIFFERENT SCENARIOS USING A SPREADSHEET MODEL

Many modellers recognize that the greatest asset of the spreadsheet is its 'user-friendliness' and its ability to facilitate end-user experimentation. Previous chapters have taken a step-by-step approach to describing how the spreadsheet can be utilized in the development of a formal business model. In contrast, this chapter will describe a number of ways in which the end user may experiment with a formal business model, and, in doing so, be able to consider and quantify a variety of possible outcomes for the problem under consideration. If this experimentation is performed sensibly, the end user may be afforded with a greater insight into a business problem and its possible solutions.

Readers with limited modelling experience may ask, 'Why experiment?' or 'Why consider a number of scenarios?' The answer to these questions is simple: businesses operate in an uncertain world where the price of goods, costs of raw materials or the interest rate charged by a bank are subject to change.

If money is borrowed by taking out a personal loan with a bank, then the interest charged by the bank may be variable. If a model is built to calculate the monthly repayment and assumes an interest rate of 15 per cent, then the resultant solution provided by the model (i.e. the monthly repayment) represents only one possible scenario for the borrower. In contrast, interest rates may vary between 13 per cent and 16 per cent, and, as a consequence, it may be useful if the model provides monthly repayments corresponding to the various interest rates which may be charged.

Equally, the borrower may only wish to pay a certain amount each month to repay the loan. In this case, it may be useful to use a formal model and supporting spreadsheet tools to start with the desired model output (the monthly repayment) and 'calculate backwards' to determine the required input (the corresponding rate of interest).

Finally, the model user may wish to compare a number of modelling situations or *scenarios* by creating a table listing the values for the model's parameters and resultant output for each scenario. If a model has been built to compare a variety of production strategies, the end user can readily identify the 'best' solution in terms of, say, cost minimization, or be aware of the difference in output for the proposed situations.

If experimentation is carried out by a model user with limited spreadsheet experience, the necessary analysis can be greatly simplified if the model is based on a formal structure (i.e. the model's input, calculations and output are distinct). Moreover, a formal spreadsheet model should always provide the end user with navigational facilities to ensure easy inspection of the model's output, as well as access to the input screens so that the values of input parameters can be easily changed. This has been described with reference to a formal model structure earlier in the chapter.

In particular, Excel offers three powerful tools which can be used to facilitate user experimentation. The tools are:

- Data Table
- Goal Seek
- Scenario Manager

In this chapter, each tool will be applied to a formal business model which depicts a company's six-monthly cash flow.

In general, the most common types of 'formal' experimentation which may be undertaken with the aid of a business model are:

- Model optimization
- Sensitivity and 'what if' analysis

Model optimization involves identifying the best answer to the problem under consideration (e.g. identifying the product mix from a production run which minimizes company costs), whereas 'what if' analysis is the process whereby a number of possible scenarios can be explored with the end user paying attention to the impact of these changes on the model's output. Many modern spreadsheets incorporate powerful built-in functions which facilitate both types of experimentation. In particular, both sensitivity analysis and model optimization can be undertaken by utilizing the data table facility which is provided by most modern spreadsheets.

THE DATA TABLE

A data table is a built-in spreadsheet facility which provides a record of the change in value of a model's output in response to changes in the values of one or two of its input variables. This record can help the end user identify the optimal or 'best' possible solution to a modelling situation and also demonstrate how variable or sensitive the model solution is to changes in the values of the selected input parameters.

In general, a data table can be incorporated easily into a formal model which is based on a block structure. It is good practice to locate each data table within its own self-contained screen(s) (depending upon its size), preferably adjacent to the model's main set of results. Moreover, ease of navigation between the separate sections of the formal model will help to increase the 'what if' capability of the model and, in turn, enhance the potential effectiveness of any resultant decisions.

The following section of this chapter outlines the 'mechanics' of constructing a data table. This is achieved by considering a simple cashflow model. In this example the data table is used to measure the change in the company's end-of-period balance with respect to changes in value of certain input variables. The Data Table facility offered by Microsoft Excel is described and the description provided details the construction of the cashflow model and use of the Data Table facility. This should be useful not only to modellers who use Excel but also to those who employ other spreadsheets since the steps described are readily transferable. In previous chapters, the simple 'contractor's' model was considered. Because of the small number of relatively basic calculations undertaken and the end-user requirements from this particular model, the inclusion of a data table to facilitate either model optimization or 'what if' analysis is inappropriate. As a consequence, an alternative problem (i.e. a company's cashflow) will be studied instead.

TESTING THE SENSITIVITY OF A MODEL'S OUTPUT

Sensitivity analysis involves determining the extent that a model's output may vary by altering the values of one or more of its input parameters. In measuring the sensitivity of a model's output, the end user undertakes 'what if' analysis. 'What if' analysis is the process whereby a number of possible scenarios (as depicted by the values that the input variables take) can be explored by utilizing a formal business model. Specifically, this analysis serves two main purposes:

- It demonstrates the variability of a model's results, and in turn the sensitivity of a business decision, with respect to changes in the value of one or more input parameters.
- It shows the degree of confidence an end user can have in the decisions implemented in response to a model's output. Scenarios can be considered which otherwise may be either too expensive or impractical.

The next part of this chapter will demonstrate how a data table can be used to assist in both of these areas by making reference to a specific business application, and the reader will also be able to use the data table as a tool for measuring a model's sensitivity by answering the case study questions at the end of the chapter.

THE CASHFLOW MODEL

A medium-sized manufacturing company has recently encountered cashflow problems. To avoid these problems occurring in the future, the accounts manager would like to develop a formal spreadsheet model which can be used to predict six-monthly cashflows. In response, a formal cashflow model has been developed using Microsoft Excel, which displays the opening and closing balance at the end of each month up to the end of July 1994. The cashflow model has been developed using the following assumptions:

- Opening balance on 1st March is £3500.
- Each unit sold is priced at £19.75. All of the sales made are on a credit basis where debtors are given two months credit.
- A bank loan of £8000 is taken out in April.
- Raw materials cost £5.00 per unit. Eighty per cent of this cost is paid in the month of production, and the remainder in the following month.
- Direct labour costs £10.00 per unit and this cost is met in the month of production.
- Variable expenses are £3.50 per unit, of which 25 per cent are paid in the month of production and the remainder in the following month.
- Fixed costs of £700 are paid each month.
- A bill of £18 000 for new machinery will be paid in May.

The input screen corresponding to this model is shown in Figure 8.2. For the sake of simplicity, the model displayed does not include any introduction, help or macro facilities. If the model was to be implemented by an end user with limited knowledge of spreadsheets, these facilities would obviously be included. However, this chapter focuses on model sensitivity, and so will only consider the input, calculation and output sections that would be included in this type of formal model.

In the input screen shown in Figure 8.2, all of the variables and assumptions have been listed. The process screen which is shown in Figure 8.3 contains formulae which reference the relevant cells located in the input screen. Moreover, for the sake of presentation, the cost/price data, model assumptions and the units sold/produced are kept separate within the input screen.

Because reference has been made to cells in the input screen, the end user can experiment 'informally' by changing selected cells on the screen shown in Figure 8.2. By navigating to the process ('model') screen shown in Figure 8.3, the model user can record the effect of these informal changes.

Figure 8.3 displays the cashflow analysis. The information shown on the screen allows the accounts manager to predict whether the company has sufficient cash to stay in business. Within the model screen shown in Figure 8.3, the following names and formulae have been used:

Named cells: C5   RAWCOST
               C6   VARCOST
               C7   LABCOST
               C9   FIXED

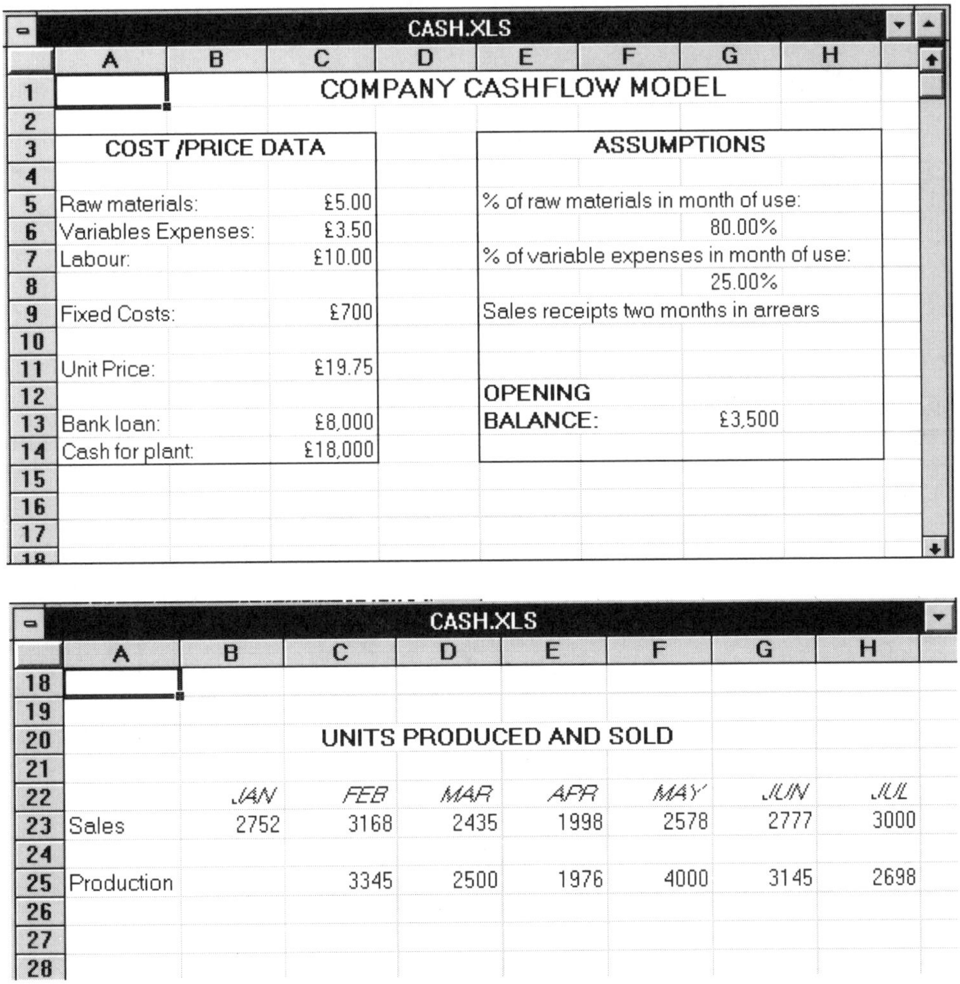

CASH.XLS

	A	B	C	D	E	F	G	H
1			COMPANY CASHFLOW MODEL					
2								
3	COST /PRICE DATA				ASSUMPTIONS			
4								
5	Raw materials:		£5.00		% of raw materials in month of use:			
6	Variables Expenses:		£3.50				80.00%	
7	Labour:		£10.00		% of variable expenses in month of use:			
8							25.00%	
9	Fixed Costs:		£700		Sales receipts two months in arrears			
10								
11	Unit Price:		£19.75					
12					OPENING			
13	Bank loan:		£8,000		BALANCE:		£3,500	
14	Cash for plant:		£18,000					
15								
16								
17								

CASH.XLS

	A	B	C	D	E	F	G	H
18								
19								
20			UNITS PRODUCED AND SOLD					
21								
22		*JAN*	*FEB*	*MAR*	*APR*	*MAY*	*JUN*	*JUL*
23	Sales	2752	3168	2435	1998	2578	2777	3000
24								
25	Production		3345	2500	1976	4000	3145	2698
26								
27								
28								

Figure 8.2 The input screen for the cashflow model

C11	PRICE
C13	LOAN
C14	PLANTCOST
G6	PERCRAW
G8	PERCVAR
G13	OPENBAL

Cash receipts for March (M8)	**=K8*$PRICE**
Total receipts for March (M11)	**=SUM(M8:M9)**
Fixed costs	**=$FIXED**
Raw materials for February (L17)	**=$RAWCOST*$PERCVAR*L14**
Variable expenses February (L18)	**=$VARCOST*$PERCVAR*L14**
Direct labour (L19)	**=$LABCOST*L14**
Raw materials for March (M17)	**=$RAWCOST*((1–$PERCRAW)*L14+$PERCRAW*M14)**

	CASH.XLS						
	J	K	L	M	N	O	P	Q
1	CASHFLOW ANALYSIS - 19X4							
2	28/11/94							
3	MONTH		*JAN*	*FEB*	*MAR*	*APR*	*MAY*	*JUN*	*JUL*
4								
5	Cash Inflows:							
6	Sales (units)		2752	3168	2435	1998	2578	2777	3000
7								
8	*Cash Receipts*				£54,352	£62,568	£48,091	£39,461	£50,916
9	*Other Receipts*				£8,000				
10								
11	TOTAL RECEIPTS:				£54,352	£70,568	£48,091	£39,461	£50,916
12								
13	Cash Outflows:							
14	Production (units)			3345	2500	1976	4000	3145	2698
15								
16	*FixedCosts*			£700	£700	£700	£700	£700	£700
17	*Raw Materials*			£13380	£13345	£10404	£17976	£16580	£13937
18	*Variable expenses*			£2927	£10968	£8292	£8687	£13252	£10616

	CASH.XLS						
	J	K	L	M	N	O	P	Q
18	*Variable expenses*		£2927	£10968	£8292	£8687	£13252	£10616
19	*Direct labour*		£33450	£25000	£19760	£40000	£31450	£26980
20	*Other Expenses*				£18000			
21								
22	TOTAL PAYMENTS			£50013	£39156	£85363	£61982	£52233
23								
24	Opening Balance			£3500	£7839	£39251	£1980	-£20542
25	Closing balance			£7839	£39251	£1980	-£20542	-£21860
26								

Figure 8.3 The process screen for the cashflow model

Variable expenses for March (M18) = **\$VARCOST*((1–\$PERCVAR)*L14+**
                                      \$PERCVAR*M14)
Total expenses (M22)   = **SUM(M16:M20)**
Closing balance for March   = **M24+M11–M22**

Obviously, if a formal cashflow model is being developed, it is useful to use named cells and ranges in the formulae used, for the reasons described in Chapter 4.

Inspection of the model indicates a worsening closing balance for the manufacturing company; i.e. as time goes on, the closing balance becomes increasingly negative. By experimenting in the informal manner described earlier, the model user can determine the values of unit selling price, unit labour cost and raw material cost which may help to reduce this particular problem.

However, this analysis may be undertaken more formally by using the Data Table facility to record the effect on end-of-period balance (July 1994) with respect to changes in value of these particular input variables.

There are two types of data table which may be constructed using Excel: a *one-input* data table and a *two-input* data table. With a one-input table, values are entered into the spreadsheet corresponding to one input variable and their effect is recorded in tabular form. With a two-input table, the effect on a model's output is recorded for changes in two input variables.

For the cashflow model under consideration, both a one-input and a two-input data table have been used to measure the sensitivity of the company's end-of-period balance with respect to changes in value for certain input variables. A description of how to construct the two types of table is provided below.

Constructing a one-input data table

Using either a column or row, enter the chosen values for the input variable. In the example of the one-input data table shown in Figure 8.4, the data table has been used to measure the influence of proportion of variable expenses paid in the month of production on the end-of-period balance. The chosen values for this variable are 10%, 15%, ... , 60%, although in practice there is no limit in this facility on the number of values which may be considered.

Arbitrarily, a column arrangement has been chosen for the one-input data table presented in Figure 8.4. Using this arrangement, the formulae representing the output variable should be entered above the first value (of the uncompleted data table) and one cell to the right of the column of values. One advantage of using the one-input data table in Excel is that more than one output variable can be considered within a single table, the additional formulae being entered on the same row and to the right of the first formula.

To complete the calculations for each value of the input variable, the rectangular range of cells containing the values and formula should be selected, i.e. K30:L41. The end user must then select:

Data
Table

The Excel window corresponding to the Data Table facility is shown in Figure 8.5. Since the column arrangement has been chosen, the reference to the input cell (percentage of variable expense paid in the month of production) , G8, must be entered into the column input box.

	J	K	L	M	N	O	P	Q	
27	SENSITIVITY ANALYSIS:			*one-input data table*					
28									
29			*Final Balance*						
30			-£21860		*This table measures the effect of chan*				
31		10%	-£22199		*the proportion of variable expenses p*				
32		15%	-£22086		*the month of production on the end of*				
33			20%	-£21973		*balance.*			
34	% Var	25%	-£21860						
35	expense	30%	-£21746						
36		35%	-£21633						
37		40%	-£21520						
38		45%	-£21407						
39		50%	-£21294						
40		55%	-£21180						
41		60%	-£21067						
42									
43									

Figure 8.4   Output from a one-input data table

Within a formal business model, each variable should be named (as mentioned earlier in the chapter), and as a consequence the variable name PERCVAR could be entered instead of its equivalent cell reference. Finally, after selecting **OK**, Excel enters each value displayed on the table into the model and fills the table with the corresponding results. Figure 8.4 shows the completed data table. It should be apparent that, by changing the proportion of variable expenses paid in the month of production, little change occurs in the company's end-of-period balance. Nevertheless, eleven calculations have been undertaken quickly and automatically, and the model user is provided with both an insight and permanent record of the behaviour of this particular input variable.

Constructing a two-input data table

If the model user wishes to determine the effect of changing *two* variables on a model's output, a two-input data table can be used. In Figure 8.6 a two-input data table has been constructed measuring the change in end-of-period balance for a range of unit selling prices and labour costs.

To set up this table, the output formula should be entered onto the spreadsheet. The cell containing this formula represents the top left-hand corner of the two-input data table. In the column below this formula, the values corresponding to one of the variables will be entered, while the values corresponding to the other variable are entered in the cells immediately to the right of the formula.

Again, to complete the calculations for each value of the input variable, the rectangular range of cells containing the values and formula should be selected, i.e. K58:Q69. The end user must then select:

<u>D</u>ata
<u>T</u>able

and select both the row and column input cells either by name or cell reference. As mentioned previously, the window corresponding to the Data Table facility is shown in Figure 8.5, and the completed data table is illustrated in Figure 8.6.

Once this table has been completed, the model user will be able to identify the effect of changing both unit price and labour cost on the end-of-period balance. Inspection of the completed data table shows that the negative cash flow can be reduced by increasing unit price. However, the model user should be aware that volume of sales has been kept constant, and the impact of an increase in unit price on volume sales has not been quantified within the scenarios presented by the data table. These issues should influence the range of values for labour cost and selling price considered in the data table.

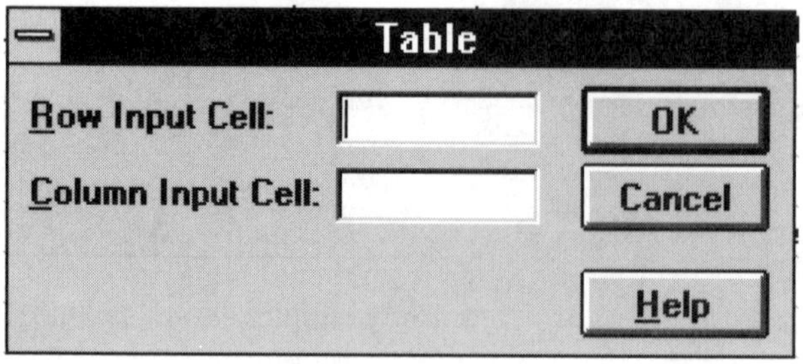

Figure 8.5 Excel window used to activate the data table

	J	K	L	M	N	O	P	Q	R
53									
54	SENSITIVITY ANALYSIS:			*two-input data table*					
55									
56									
57		*Final Balance*		**Unit labour cost**					
58		-£21860	£10.00	£10.50	£11.00	£11.50	£12.00	£12.50	£13.00
59		£15.00	-83282	-90441	-97601	-104760	-111920	-119079	-126239
60		£15.50	-76816	-83976	-91135	-98295	-105454	-112614	-119773
61		£16.00	-70351	-77510	-84670	-91829	-98989	-106148	-113308
62		£16.50	-63885	-71045	-78204	-85364	-92523	-99683	-106842
63		£17.00	-57420	-64579	-71739	-78898	-86058	-93217	-100377
64	Unit price	£17.50	-50954	-58114	-65273	-72433	-79592	-86752	-93911
65		£18.00	-44489	-51648	-58808	-65967	-73127	-80286	-87446
66		£18.50	-38023	-45183	-52342	-59502	-66661	-73821	-80980
67		£19.00	-31558	-38717	-45877	-53036	-60196	-67355	-74515
68		£19.50	-25092	-32252	-39411	-46571	-53730	-60890	-68049
69		£20.00	-18627	-25786	-32946	-40105	-47265	-54424	-61584
70									

Figure 8.6 Output from a two-input data table

Moreover, if any additional input variables are changed, e.g. unit raw material cost or volume sales, then the results stored in the Excel data table will alter automatically. This response is different from the data table facility offered by Lotus 1-2-3, where the Data Table command would have to be re-invoked in order to re-calculate the values of the selected output variable.

Finally, if the data table is to be incorporated within a formal business model, its presentation will be of utmost importance. The presentation of results stored in a data table can be enhanced by formatting the output cells of the data table in the most appropriate way, prior to any calculations being undertaken. In both the one-input data table shown in Figure 8.4 and the two-input data table presented in Figure 8.6, this has been achieved using the Excel commands:

Format
Number

and selecting Number from the Category box.

Additionally, any data table screens used within a formal structure should be documented by including screen titles, user instructions and, if necessary, an explanation on how to implement the results.

MODEL OPTIMIZATION

As stated, model optimization involves identifying the 'best' answer to the problem under consideration, and, in practice, this may involve either maximizing or minimizing a particular business function, typically maximizing revenue or minimizing cost. If the data table has been used to identify a best solution based on either of these criteria, its application will generally involve the end user identifying either the smallest or largest value from the table and recording the corresponding values of the input variables being considered. For example, the spreadsheet may be applied to a production problem, in which case maximizing or minimizing a particular outcome may be a common application.

GOALSEEKING

When a model is used to solve a particular business problem, the end user usually starts with values of its model's input variables and records the corresponding model output. However, it is often useful to determine the required input which would yield either a desired or known output from a model. Microsoft Excel and a number of other spreadsheets offer an additional 'what if' facility called goalseek, which can be used to perform this type of 'backward' calculation. In general three parameters need to be specified when using a goalseek facility:

INPUT or SET cell   the cell to be varied
OUTPUT or CHANGING cell   which will contain the known or desired result
DESIRED result or VALUE of SET cell

When using the goalseek facility, the spreadsheet varies the value in the specified input cell until the dependent formula (i.e. the output cell) returns the desired result.

In the cashflow model considered in this chapter, the accounts manager may decide that an end-of-period balance of −£10 000 is acceptable. In order to achieve this balance, it has been agreed that unit selling price should be increased, since the company has determined that if the increase is not excessive, any price change will not adversely effect volume sales. That is, the model user starts with a predetermined value of the output variable, year-end balance (i.e. −£10 000), and works backwards to calculate the necessary input, i.e. unit price.

To determine the unit price which will yield this end balance, the model user must select:

Formula
Goal Seek

which results in the Goal Seek window shown in Figure 8.7 appearing on the screen.

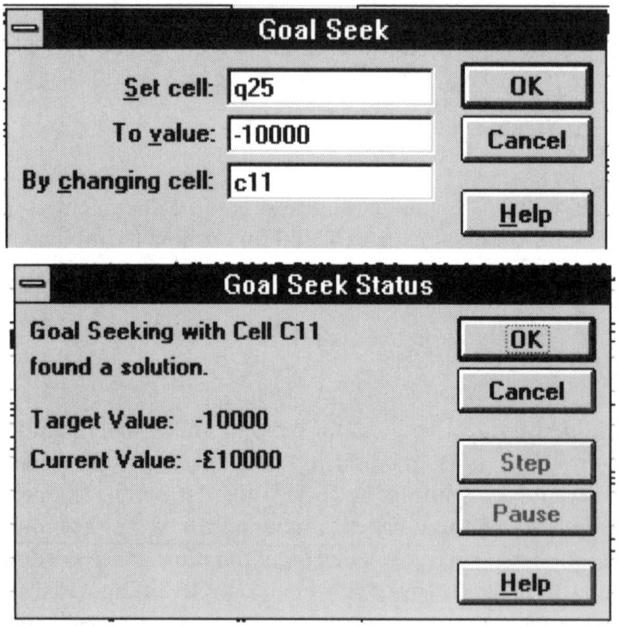

Figure 8.7 Excel's Goal Seek window

	CASH.XLS								
	A	B	C	D	E	F	G	H	
1			COMPANY CASHFLOW MODEL						
2									
3	COST /PRICE DATA				ASSUMPTIONS				
4									
5	Raw materials:		£5.00		% of raw materials in month of use:				
6	Variables Expenses:		£3.50				80.00%		
7	Labour:		£10.00		% of variable expenses in month of use:				
8							25.00%		
9	Fixed Costs:		£700		Sales receipts two months in arrears				
10									
11	Unit Price:		£20.67						
12					OPENING				
13	Bank loan:		£8,000		BALANCE:		£3,500		
14	Cash for plant:		£18,000						
15									
16									

	CASH.XLS								
	J	K	L	M	N	O	P	Q	R
21									
22	TOTAL PAYMENTS			£50013	£39156	£85363	£61982	£52233	
23									
24	Opening Balance			£3500	£10363	£44681	£9642	-£11047	
25	Closing balance			£10363	£44681	£9642	-£11047	-£10000	
26									

Figure 8.8   Cashflow model after using the Goal Seek facility

In the Set cell box, **Q25** (or the name **YEBAL**) should be entered, since we require this value to be fixed. The value −**10000** is then entered in the To value box. Finally **C11** (or **PRICE**) should be entered in the By changing cell box.

If a solution can be determined, the required results will be displayed on the screen. Alternatively, if the original model is required, the end user may **Cancel** from the Goal Seek facility.

Finally, if no solution exists, Excel will display an appropriate message on the screen. Figure 8.8 shows the model screen after the Goal Seek facility has been used, displaying the desired end-of-period balance of −£10 000. Inspection of the model's input screen indicated that the desired end-of-period balance can be achieved with a unit selling price of £20.67.

ANALYSING SCENARIOS WITHIN A FORMAL MODEL

The final 'what if' tool provided by Excel to be described in this chapter is the Scenario Manager facility. Quite simply, a scenario is a group of input values provided by the model user which represent either a likely or proposed business situation. Excel can record either an individual or group of scenarios, permitting the user to view the results when considering an individual scenario or create a report which *summarizes* all input values and corresponding output for each scenario created.

	Best	*Scenario* *Worst*	*Most likely*
RAWCOST	£3.00	£6.50	£4.50
VARCOST	£3.00	£4.00	£3.50
LABCOST	£9.50	£12.00	£10.50
PRICE	£21.00	£18.00	£19.75

Figure 8.9   Different scenarios for the cashflow model

To create a scenario, the end user must decide which input variables to consider and select an output variable which is dependent upon these parameters. For the cashflow model considered in this chapter, it may be appropriate for the accounts manager to define the 'best', 'worst' and 'most likely' scenarios. The advantage of using the scenario manager is that the value of more than two input variables can be considered at the same time. These scenarios are presented in Figure 8.9.

If a block structure has been used during the development of the model (as defined in Chapter 3), the process of creating scenarios is much simplified because the input variables will be located together and will be separate and self-contained from the rest of the model. To create a set of scenarios, the user should select:

Formula
Scenario Manager

which results in a window appearing on the screen like that shown in Figure 8.10.

To enter an individual scenario, the input cells (i.e. raw material, variable expenses, etc.) should be recorded in the Changing Cells box. The **Add** and **Name** options should then be activated to define (enter the values for each variable under consideration) and name a particular scenario.

To use a particular scenario, the **Show** option within the Scenario Manager facility must be selected. The input values corresponding to the chosen scenario will appear within the appropriate cells in the spreadsheet model, and, in turn, the model will be re-calculated in response to these new values.

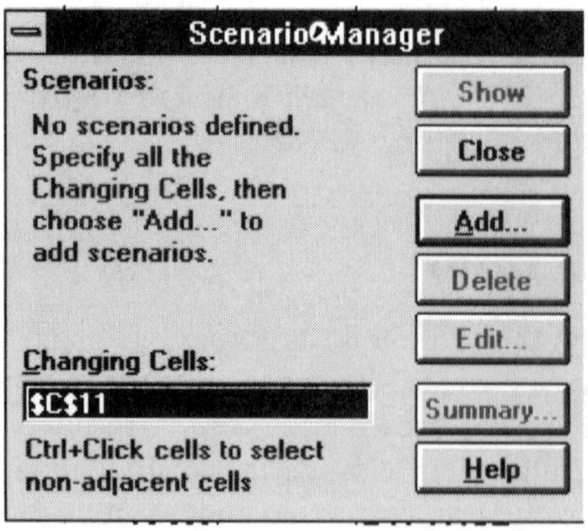

Figure 8.10   The Scenario Manager window

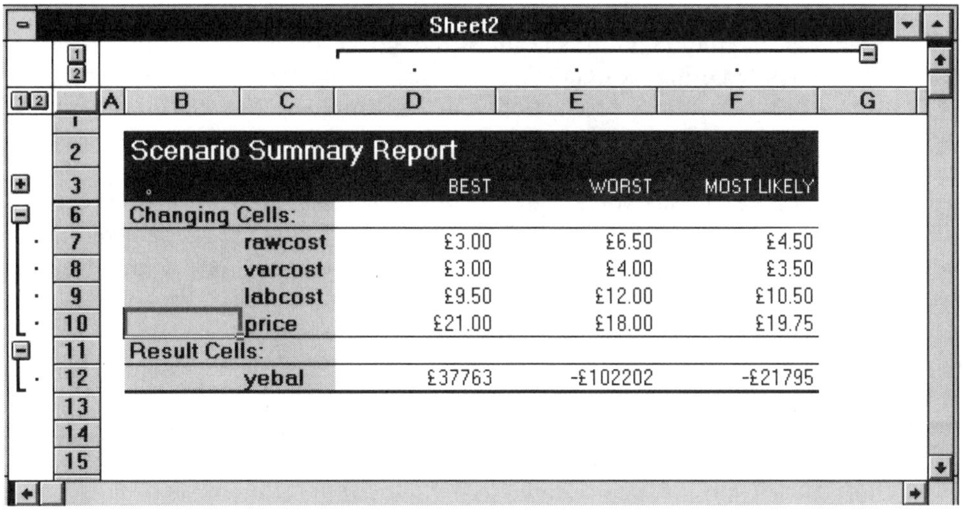

Figure 8.11   Report generated by Excel's Scenario Manager

Finally, by selecting the **Summary** option within the Scenario Manager facility, the model user can define the output variables to be considered (in this case the year-end balance for the cash flow YEBAL) and can subsequently create a report, in this case providing the results for the selected 'best', 'worst' and 'most likely' scenarios. The report generated for the cashflow model is presented in Figure 8.11 and is housed on its own spreadsheet, separate from the main model. In turn the sheet housing the report can be saved and printed. By creating the table on a separate sheet, the end user does not have to worry about overwriting any of the model's contents during the process of experimentation.

CONCLUSIONS

Previous chapters of this book have described a more formal approach to spreadsheet model-ling, whereas in this chapter a greater emphasis has been placed on the experimental facilities offered by the spreadsheet. In practice, there may be a trade-off between end-user experimenta-tion (afforded by facilities such as Data Table, Goal Seek and Scenario Manager) and the formality required in many modelling applications. Without conflict, end-user interaction and experimentation can be incorporated into a structured model. To ensure the effectiveness of any 'what if' analysis, the modeller must recognize that the end user should be able to navigate between the input, process and output screens housed in the formal structure. In more complex models, particularly those with a larger number of input variables, total automation of the 'what if' facilities may infringe on this end-user interaction and experimentation. In such situations, it may be better to only part automate the modelling process and provide the end user with comprehensive instructions regarding the suitability and use of the various 'what if' tools. In short, automation of the facilities described should be dictated both by end-user requirements and capabilities and the complexity of the situation being modelled.

In particular, three 'what if' tools were considered in this chapter:

- Data table
- Goalseek
- Scenario manager

The first tool to be considered was the data table, which can be used to record the impact of changing one or two input variables on the output of the model. In this chapter the change in year-end balance was recorded using the data table in response to changes in value of percentage of variable costs paid in the month of production and also for changes in unit price and unit labour cost. In contrast, the goalseek facility is particularly useful if the model user needs to determine the required input which would yield either a desired or known output from a model, i.e. the user starts with the result and works back to find the necessary input. The last 'what if' tool described was the scenario manager facility. This facility can be used to produce results for a range of different data sets, and, if required, display these results in the form of an on-screen report. One obvious set of scenarios which may arranged in this way are 'best', 'worst' and 'most likely' outcomes for the problem under consideration.

However, it should be obvious that when determining a best solution from a model, or measuring the sensitivity of a model's output using any of the facilities described, the end user should always remember that the model developed is only a simplification of reality and care should be taken in determining the possible scenarios and values for each input variable under consideration. Specifically, the model should be used to support the end user's judgement, not replace it. In particular, there may exist a number of qualitative factors which require individual consideration. Such factors may be influenced by events inside the organization, e.g. potential problems with industrial relations, or events external to the organization, such as government policy or competition from other organizations. In practice, the output from the (spreadsheet) model may have to be modified judgementally in response to these factors.

REVIEW QUESTIONS

1. Why is it necessary for a user to experiment with a formal business model?
2. Explain why the process of using a formal model to explore different scenarios is greatly simplified when a spreadsheet model has been developed using a formal structure.
3. Why is it often necessary to incorporate a facility which affords end-user experimentation within a structured spreadsheet model.
4. What is meant by the term 'model optimization'?
5. What is meant by the terms 'model sensitivity' and 'what if' analysis?
6. Describe the features of the data table.
7. What design factors must be considered when including a data table within a formal spreadsheet model? (*Hint*: consider the model's block structure, spreadsheet documentation and data table presentation.)
8. What is meant by the term 'goalseeking'?
9. Describe the general features of a 'goalseek' facility.
10. What is a business scenario? Which scenarios are most likely to be considered by the end user of a formal business model?
11. Describe the general features of the Scenario Manager facility offered by Excel.
12. *Briefly* describe the factors which will influence whether the 'what if' tools described in this chapter should be partly or fully automated when incorporated into a formal spreadsheet model.

CASE STUDY QUESTIONS

1. The end user is interested in determining how sensitive the net present value (NPV) of the investment is to changes in unit selling price (£) and annual growth rate (per cent). Using the

formal model developed, measure the sensitivity of the NPV using a data table. After discussion with the end user, it has been decided that a realistic range of unit selling prices is £6 to £10.50, and the growth rate of sales is estimated to be between −3 per cent and +5 per cent.

2. The end user does not require a fully automated spreadsheet model. However, the model user has only a limited knowledge of spreadsheets, and, as a consequence, comprehensive user instructions need to be written to support the use of the data table facility. Write a set of instructions which describe how a data table should be constructed and how the output should be used to measure the model's sensitivity.

3. The end user is also interested in determining the rate of interest (per cent) which results in the investment breaking even (i.e. returns an NPV of zero). Write a set of comprehensive user instructions which describe how this calculation may be undertaken using the goalseek facility.

4. It is necessary to incorporate in the model the following 'best', 'worst' and 'most likely' scenarios. Use the scenario facility to build these scenarios and provide a results screen to house the output provide by this particular facility.

		Scenarios	
	Best	Worst	Most likely
Selling price	12.50	6.00	8.50
Unit cost	5.00	7.00	6.50
Investment	15 000	22 000	20 000
Discount rate	7%	14%	12%

Again, provide suitable user instructions.

NINE

ADDITIONAL ISSUES IN SPREADSHEET MODELLING

OVERVIEW

This chapter describes a number of additional modelling concepts which do not fit easily into the main chapters of the book. These features should generally be considered after the formal model has been developed and consider both aspects of model presentation and security.

OBJECTIVES

After reading this chapter and working through the questions, the reader will be able to:

- Recognize the usefulness of investing time in model presentation.
- Use large, bold and italic text for section titles within the formal model structure.
- Enhance the display of an Excel model by hiding the spreadsheet's gridlines and row and column headings.
- Use boxes, lines and shading to enhance the appearance of the spreadsheet.
- Recognize the need to protect the spreadsheet code included in a model.
- Understand the importance of data security and be able to secure a model using passwords.

INTRODUCTION

There are a number of modelling concepts which do not neatly fit into the interrelated steps which form the basis of this book. These concepts include the issues of model presentation and both model and data security. When a model has been developed for use by an end user with little knowledge of spreadsheets, these features are of great importance. This chapter is divided into two sections: the first deals with model presentation, and the second with aspects of security. The issues discussed will be similar for the majority of non-trivial modelling applications developed using Microsoft Excel and, in order to demonstrate their application, reference will be made to the simple, but formal, 'contractor's' model.

SPREADSHEET PRESENTATION

In a formal spreadsheet model there are five main ways in which the appearance of the model can be enhanced. A formal model may be enhanced by:

- Altering font sizes and text styles on the spreadsheet
- Providing on-screen (spreadsheet) documentation
- Removing row and column headings and gridlines
- Altering font sizes and text styles on the spreadsheet
- Using boxes, lines and shading to enhance the appearance of the spreadsheet

Altering font sizes and text styles on the spreadsheet

By allowing the modeller to alter the size and type of text, the appearance of a business model developed using Microsoft Excel can be made to resemble (as best as possible) the report format of the client organization. In Excel the modeller can increase or reduce the size of text, as well as making it bold and/or italics, by using the icons present on the spreadsheet's toolbar. These icons are shown in Figure 9.1.

In the 'contractor's' model, the modeller enhanced the appearance of the title for each separate block in the model by using the Bold facility. Moreover, it is also possible (as indicated in Figure 9.1) to make these titles larger than the general text which is resident on each screen. However, if the size of a title is increased, then the row in which it is resident also increases in size and, in turn, this may affect the dimensions of the individual block. If larger titles are required on each model screen, then it is good practice to incorporate these at the time when the block's dimensions are being defined.

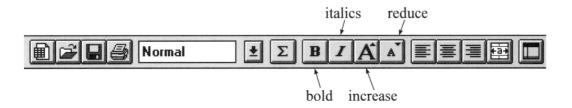

Figure 9.1   Icons for enhancing the appearance of text from the utility toolbar

On-screen (spreadsheet) documentation

The spreadsheet or on-screen documentation of a formal spreadsheet model takes the form of informative statements written in English within each self-contained block which may be accessed by the model user. This type of documentation was described fully in Chapter 7. The purpose of the statements is to provide support to an end user who wishes to understand the role of the code contained within the model and also to support those modelling personnel who are responsible for the future maintenance and support of the model.

Moreover, it is also useful to provide comments on the spreadsheet which will enhance its appearance and assist the end user. In particular, the modeller can add comments in boxes using Excel by utilizing the facilities incorporated in the spreadsheet's Drawing toolbar (in particular the Text box and Arrow tools). In Figure 9.2 a comment written inside a box has been included on the model's results screen, highlighting the cost of a particular building contract.

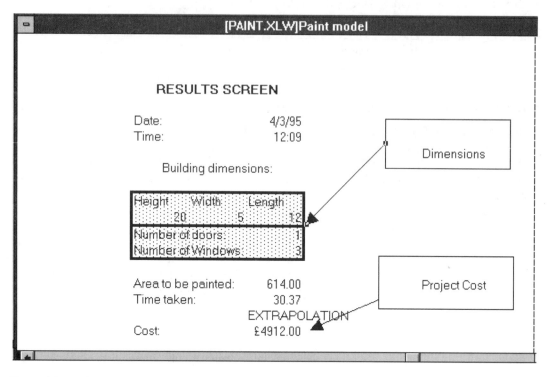

Figure 9.2   Using comments within a formal spreadsheet model

Removal of gridlines and row and column headings

One common characteristic of Excel (and most other spreadsheets) is the gridlines and the row and column headings which define the cells on the spreadsheet. Many end users who utilize a spreadsheet model written in Excel may have limited computer experience, and, as a consequence, would perhaps prefer a formal model which is more user-friendly in appearance. An easy way of enhancing the appearance of a model is by removing both the gridlines and row and column headings from the spreadsheet. A comparison has been made below in Figures 9.3 and 9.4, which show the introduction screen of the 'contractor's' model before and after these changes have been made.

In Microsoft Excel row and column headings can be removed by activating:

<u>O</u>ptions
<u>D</u>isplay

and switching off (by clicking on and removing the cross ×) the gridlines and row and column headings facilities. In the 'contractor's' model, this was achieved by writing an Auto_Open macro (see Chapter 5) which included the statement:

= DISPLAY(FALSE,FALSE,FALSE,TRUE,0,,TRUE,FALSE,1)

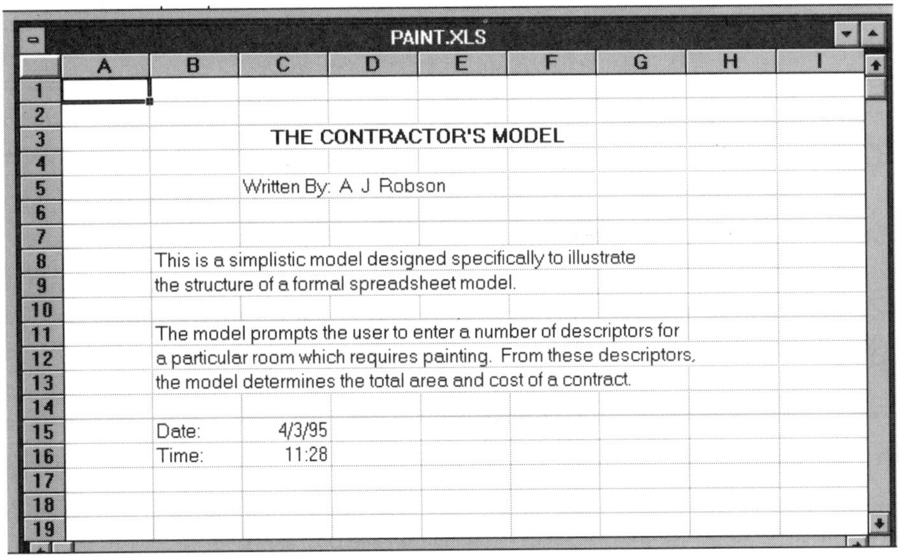

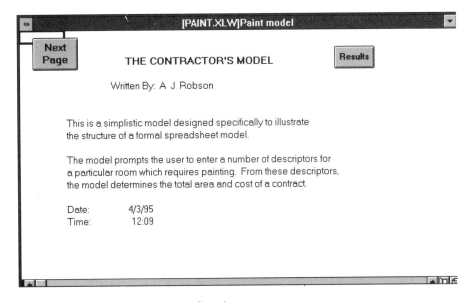

Figure 9.3   An introduction screen before changes

Figure 9.4   An introduction screen after changes

which ensured that the model had the required user-friendly appearance on retrieval. Additionally, it is also good practice to ensure that the cursor is located on the introduction screen (usually in the top left-hand corner of the model) and that the window is of an appropriate size (i.e. so that each model screen fits exactly into it) on model retrieval. Again, the appropriate command can be incorporated into the Auto_Open macro, namely:

$$= \textbf{FORMULA.GOTO("R1C1")}$$

and

$$= WINDOW.SIZE(491.25,287.25)$$

respectively.

Using boxes, lines and shading on a spreadsheet

The screens accessed most often by the model user can be enhanced further still by using boxes, lines and shading on the spreadsheet. In order to put a border (i.e. lines or box) around a block of cells, the modeller must first highlight the cells and then select:

Format
Border

The border chosen may be any combination of vertical and horizontal lines located to the left, right, top or bottom of the cell and, moreover, may be single or double lines. The choice of border will be influenced by the needs of the end user and the style of the organization's general report format. In the same way, a block of cells may be shaded by activating:

Format
Patterns

In Figure 9.5, shading and borders have been added to the results screen of the 'contractor's' model. It should be apparent that the appearance of this screen has been greatly enhanced.

Moreover, the patterns, lines and boxes described above can also be produced in colour, which is particularly useful if the model is to be used in formal business presentations.

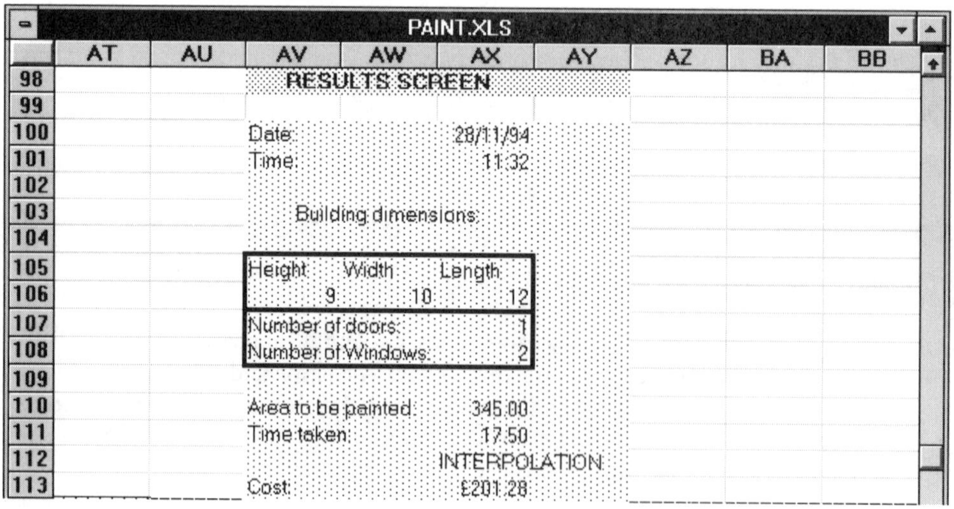

Figure 9.5 The Results screen after addition of borders and shading

MODEL ROBUSTNESS

While a formal spreadsheet model may be user-friendly and provide an effective decision-making tool, it may not stand up to an end user with little experience of spreadsheets. In particular, it is quite possible that such a model user may accidentally erase or write over some of the spreadsheet code. If the spreadsheet model is to be utilized by this type of end user, then its robustness is of utmost importance. Fortunately, most spreadsheets allow the modeller to prevent these types of accidents occurring by offering a global cell protection facility. In Excel, a spreadsheet model can be protected by activating:

<u>O</u>ptions
<u>P</u>rotect Document

which provides the modeller with a number of alternatives:

- *Password* This is used to protect the whole document and may be up to 15 characters long, but, if forgotten, the document cannot be unprotected. Moreover, the password is case-sensitive (i.e. *Contract* is a different password from *contract*).

The password can then be used to protect a chosen combination of cells, objects and windows, the default being to protect everything:

- *Cells* To protect the certain cell contents, e.g. the table of hourly rates in the 'contractor's model, this option may be switched on (by clicking on its name so that a cross, × appears) after defining the password.
- *Objects* The 'contractor's' model contained a graph to depict the relationship between contract size and duration. It also contains boxes and shading to enhance the presentation of its output screen. These features are known as objects and to ensure that they are protected, the objects option may be switched on.
- *Windows* In the 'contractor's' model, each window has been sized in order to house one screen as defined in the formal model structure. This window size may vary from PC to PC. In order to keep this constant for the 'contractor's' model, the windows option may be selected when the password is defined.

Suppose in the formal 'contractor's' model that the modeller wishes to protect everything on the spreadsheet. This may be achieved by selecting:

<u>O</u>ptions
<u>P</u>rotect Document

A cross appears as a default next to Cells, Objects and Windows. To accept this, the modeller simply needs to click **OK**. The modeller is then required to confirm the password by re-entering the selected password into the next window. If the two passwords are different, then Excel does not accept the protection. The relevant windows are displayed in Figure 9.6.

If the modeller is ever required to alter any formulae or features included in the model, then the password must be removed so that the necessary modifications take place. This can be achieved by selecting:

<u>O</u>ptions
<u>U</u>nprotect Document

Figure 9.6 Excel's password protection windows

(this is switched on in place of the Protect Document facility once the former command has been activated) and typing in the model's password. The Unprotect window is shown in Figure 9.7.

However, while all of the cells have been protected, the modeller must still ensure that the end user is able to add new data to the model. Specifically, the block of cells on the input screen must be unprotected. To achieve this, the modeller must first highlight the input range, i.e. the block W43:W51 in the 'contractor's' model, and select:

Forma̲t
Cell Protec̲tion

and turn off (by clicking on it to remove the cross ×) the Locked option. To protect the rest of the document:

O̲ptions
P̲rotect Document

should be selected as previously described.

Figure 9.7 Excel's password unprotect window

After protecting the spreadsheet in this way, an end user will be prevented from writing to any protected cells. If an attempt is made, Excel responds with a message indicating that the cells are protected. More importantly, the original contents of the 'violated' cells remain intact. However, data can still be entered to the unlocked cells situated on the model's input screen.

DATA SECURITY

The needs for data security in a number of modelling applications should be clear to most modellers and model users. Superficial data security can be provided by employing the cell protection facility offered by most spreadsheets as well as hiding confidential data. However, Microsoft Excel offers three types of more rigid security. To utilize the facilities, the modeller must select:

File

Save As

and then select **Options**.

The three types of security provided by Excel are:

- *Protection Password*   If the 'contractor's' model is to be used by a limited number of people, its security can be ensured with the use of a password. This password is particularly useful if the model houses sensitive data.

- *Write Reservation Password*   Alternatively, the users of the 'contractor's' model may only be required to use the model for calculation of new contracts, but not updating the original model. By employing a Write Reservation password, the original model cannot be updated unless an additional password is known. If the user wants to save any updated calculations, these must be saved as a different file. In particular, this password should be used to prevent an accessed model (such as a generic modelling template – see Chapter 10) being altered and re-saved.

- *Read-Only Recommended*   On certain business applications, Excel will be used to develop models which are to be inspected by an end user but not altered. This facility prompts the user that the model's contents are Read-Only. However, the facility is only a recommendation, and as a consequence, changes can still be made. If the results stored in a model must not be altered the Write Reservation password provides more robust security.

Excel's top-level security window is shown in Figure 9.8.

Obviously, the data stored in the 'contractor's' model is not greatly sensitive, and as a consequence it is unlikely that any of the higher levels of security would be used. In contrast, the global protection of the spreadsheet is particularly useful, especially if the end user has limited knowledge of spreadsheet operations.

In general, whenever passwords are used, whether it be to protect the spreadsheet, or at the top level to ensure data security, records will have to be kept of every password used. The most appropriate place to store this information would be in the model's external (or technical) documentation which will be generally used and referred to by modelling personnel. This documentation was described in Chapter 7.

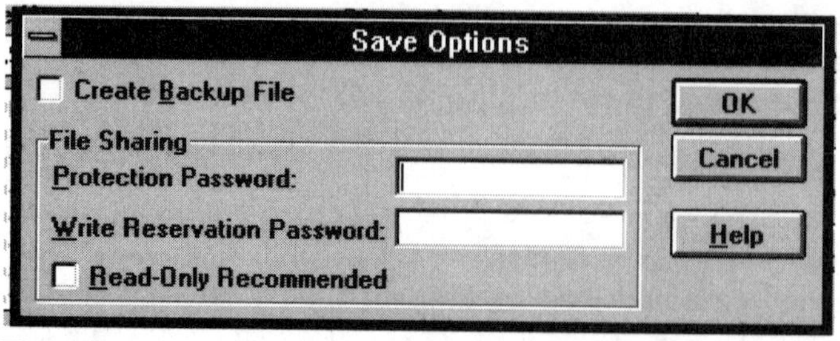

Figure 9.8   Top-level security provided by Excel

CONCLUSIONS

The concepts described in this chapter are simple, but often essential, considerations, which should be taken into account in the final stages of model development. The use of bold, italics and large print for titles, removal of gridlines and row and column headings and the location of the cursor on model retrieval are simple concepts which can serve to enhance the presentation and user-friendliness of the model.

Additionally, model robustness is very important, especially for an end user with little spreadsheet experience, and the issue of data security should be clear to both modeller and model user.

REVIEW QUESTIONS

1. Describe the five features which enhance the presentation of a spreadsheet model.
2. If large text titles are to be used for each block in a formal model, why it is important that these are input at the start of model development?
3. Comment on the importance of model robustness. Outline how this can be achieved using Microsoft Excel.
4. Describe occasions when the following types of model protection are important:
   - Password
   - Cells
   - Objects
   - Windows
5. List the important aspects of model security.
6. Describe occasions when the following types of model security are important:
   - Protection Password
   - Write Reservation
   - Read-Only Recommended.

CASE STUDY QUESTIONS

1. For the investment model, enhance the appearance of each of the screens in the model which are likely to be accessed by the model user by using:
   - Shading and boxes
   - Bold and italics for each block title
   - Comments added in boxes on the output screen

2. To ensure that the model has a user-friendly appearance on retrieval, alter the Auto_Open macro to ensure that:
   - The gridlines and row and column headings of the spreadsheet are removed
   - The size of the window fits the size of each separate screen incorporated in the model
3. Since the end user has limited spreadsheet experience, make the model as robust as possible by protecting all of the cells in the model. However, remember to unprotect the relevant cells housed in the model's input screen!
4. Assume the data is sensitive, and so enhance model security by introducing appropriate password protection.

TEN

TEMPLATES AND LIBRARIES OF CODE

OVERVIEW

If a modeller has adopted a structured approach when developing a set of spreadsheet models, it is likely that most of these models will have some common structure and content (i.e. code). This chapter identifies which areas of structure and spreadsheet code will be prevalent in most modelling applications and how a 'suite' of generic modelling templates, incorporating a degree of common code, can be developed.

OBJECTIVES

After reading this chapter and working through the questions, the reader will be able to:

- Identify a structure for a formal spreadsheet template which incorporates certain common code.
- Create a structured modelling template.
- Identify a number of applications for individual sections of spreadsheet code.
- Distinguish between code which is common to most models, complex code which may be stored in a library for further application and simpler spreadsheet code which should be generated as required.
- Recognize that a number of modelling applications may be similar, and be able to identify how a generic template or 'skeleton' model can be developed and readily customized.
- Recognize the advantages and disadvantages of using templates ('skeleton' models) and libraries of (complex) code.

INTRODUCTION

Chapter 3 described an appropriate structure for a formal spreadsheet model. This structure permits ease of navigation for an end user and ensures that the functional areas of data input, process (i.e. the 'model' block) and output remain separate and self-contained. In general, a structured model resembling Figure 10.1 should incorporate a degree of macro automation (the corresponding code will be stored on a separate, but referenced, spreadsheet as described in Chapter 5), if only to facilitate navigation between the self-contained blocks. Moreover, this automation will be common to most formal modelling applications.

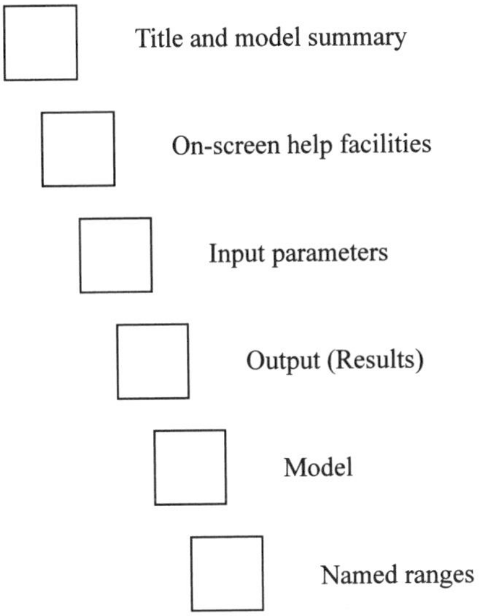

Figure 10.1   Layout for a spreadsheet model skeleton

The generic modelling template or model 'skeleton' illustrated in Figure 10.1 incorporates a number of self-contained blocks; namely introduction, help, input, output, 'model' and named ranges. Additionally, other modelling templates might incorporate blocks containing data tables, lookup tables and on-screen maps.

There are several advantages in developing a generic template before any modelling is undertaken:

- The template ensures that a consistent and formal modelling structure is adopted by the modeller or modelling team
- A standard template may help to promote a generic modelling style which is agreeable both to the modeller and end user
- Standard methods of coding can also be adopted
- Time can be saved and modelling efficiency increased because repetitive production of a model 'skeleton' and common spreadsheet code is minimized

CREATING A GENERAL MODELLING TEMPLATE

Figure 10.1 represents a structured modelling template. If the template has been newly created (i.e. it has not been produced from an existing model by removing the redundant spreadsheet code), then the block structure illustrated provides a useful formal modelling skeleton. This skeleton will facilitate effective model design because the layout ensures that the different areas of the model remain separate. The layout illustrated was described in detail in Chapter 3.

It is often useful to add to this skeleton structure a limited volume of spreadsheet code which is likely to be common to most or all modelling applications. Examples of such generic code will include:

- Navigational macros, and specifically, for more formal modelling applications, a set of macros activated by on-screen buttons.
- Titles, borders and shading for screen presentation.

- Titles, borders and shading on the results screen(s) which customizes the model output (as best possible) to the general report format of the organization. This code may also incorporate built-in functions for time and date.
- Standard details on the introduction and help blocks. Such details may include date of model creation, reference to technical assistance, top-level navigational details and general user instructions.

However, the template pictured in Figure 10.1 is not exhaustive in the range of blocks it includes. For example, there are no blocks incorporating a data table or an on-screen map. It is important to understand that certain features should only be included in the spreadsheet model if the specific modelling application dictates their inclusion. In order to maximize modeller efficiency but still maintain a standard modelling format, it may be useful for the modeller to create a suite of model templates to support a range of possible modelling applications.

CATERING FOR APPLICATIONS OF VARYING SIZE AND COMPLEXITY

In the first part of this chapter, the creation of a generic modelling template is described. The block structure adopted divides the model into a number of self-contained areas. A number of these blocks are likely to be standard for most modelling applications, e.g. user support facilities such as introduction, help and an on-screen map. In contrast, the size and content of a number of the blocks will vary according to the complexity of the modelling situation. The blocks which are likely to vary most in size are those which deal with the functional aspects of the modelling process, namely data input, process (the 'model' block) and output. In particular, it is likely to be the 'model' blocks which will be most variable in size.

In designing a template, the modeller can ensure that the variation in size of the 'model' block can be accounted for without major disruption to the structure of both the template and the standard code contained within. Specifically, if this block is located in the bottom right-hand corner of the template, as shown in Figure 10.2, then any alterations to their size, i.e. increasing

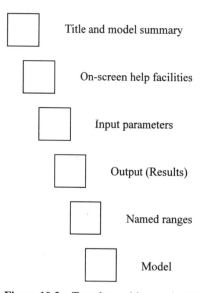

Figure 10.2 Template with a revised location for the model block

the dimensions by adding whole numbers of screens to either block, will ensure that the navigational macros (contained on a separate sheet which will be referenced by the template) still operate properly (i.e. they still navigate the end user to the appropriate place). Moreover, if particular cells or ranges of cells have been *named*, then any changes to the structure of the modelling template will not result in corruption of the relevant macro code.

CREATING TEMPLATES OF MODELS (INCLUSIVE OF CODE)

A modeller may be required to develop a 'suite' of models which are similar in content and application. For example, a modeller may develop an application providing break-even analysis for a given product manufactured by the client organization. In turn, after utilizing this particular model, the end user may be interested in obtaining similar models to provide break-even analysis for the other items produced.

In this situation, a significant proportion of the spreadsheet code contained within the first model is likely to be readily applicable to the development of any additional models. Moreover, if the modeller expects to develop a number of models based on a specific technique, then it may be useful to create a generic template incorporating the detailed spreadsheet code. However, in developing such a 'customized' template, the modeller must ensure that:

- The modelling template is as generic as possible
- The template should be responsive to any deviations in each individual application
- The template must respond to the differences in the modelling situation. However, the modelling technique and the representation of the problem should *never* be simplified in order to fit the template

COMMERCIAL MODELS

In recent times, a number of software manufacturers have developed their own models, written for particular spreadsheets and designed for specific modelling applications. A number of organizations may consider it appropriate to purchase such models. However, there are certain considerations to take into account, namely:

- The quality of the particular model and its supporting documentation
- The ability of the model to adapt to changes in a modelling situation
- The degree of informality and end-user intervention permitted by the model, if required by the end user
- The quality of model support provided by the manufacturer
- The cost and life expectancy of the program, i.e. the length of time it is expected to be relevant to the purchasing party
- The level of skill and modelling expertise available within the purchasing organization. In particular, if the organization purchasing a commercial model employs skilled modelling personnel who can develop and support a spreadsheet model both inexpensively and efficiently, there may be little point in purchasing a specific spreadsheet model

LIBRARIES OF REUSABLE CODE

This chapter has described how a general modelling template can be produced and, in turn, utilized in the development of a number of formal spreadsheet models. Moreover, this modelling skeleton may contain a proportion of generic code, including:

- Navigational macros and, in more formal templates, a macro menu or buttons
- Screen titles, borders and shading used for block presentation within the model skeleton
- Generic code used for presentation of the output screen(s) based on the standard report format of the organization
- Standard details (in skeleton form) on the introduction and help blocks, including date of model creation, reference to technical assistance, top-level navigational details and general macro instructions

In general, most modellers will have to consider a number of different modelling situations. The size and complexity of each model developed will vary between applications. When developing a model, spreadsheet code will have to be written, validated, verified and, where necessary, modified or debugged by the modeller. Consequently, a great volume of spreadsheet code may be written in a relatively short time. Moreover, modeller efficiency can be increased by minimizing the time spent repeatedly constructing and testing the same spreadsheet code. This issue is particularly relevant when creating complex spreadsheet code, which can be time-consuming. An example of complex spreadsheet code is the automated input routine shown in Figure 5.15 and reproduced here as Figure 10.3. This code, written in Excel, incorporates a number of advanced macro words and its role within the 'contractor's' model was described in Chapter 5.

Generating such a routine is time-consuming compared with constructing simple spreadsheet code. Specifically, such code requires greater debugging, testing, validating and verifying which

```
input_macro
=SELECT("R43C23")
=SELECT("R43C23:R51C23")
=CLEAR(3)
=SET.VALUE(length,"")
=SET.VALUE(height,"")
=SET.VALUE(width,"")
=SET.VALUE(windows,"")
=SET.VALUE(doors,"")
=DIALOG.BOX(input_screen)
=WHILE(OR(length<0,height<0,width<0,windows<0,doors<0))
=DIALOG.BOX(input_screen)
=NEXT()
=FORMULA(length)
=SELECT("r[2]c")
=FORMULA(height)
=SELECT("r[2]c")
=FORMULA(width)
=SELECT("r[2]c")
=FORMULA(windows)
=SELECT("r[2]c")
=FORMULA(doors)
=RETURN()
```

Figure 10.3   Excel code for an automated input routine

can be time-consuming. Because time has been invested in creating an efficient, working routine, it may be worth recording the code either on paper or on computer as a text file, so that it may be utilized within another model. Depending on the complexity of individual sections of code, it may also be useful to provide accompanying documentation, additional to any spreadsheet documentation, to define the cell references which may be variable in future applications, i.e. input cell's length, height, etc. in the routine illustrated in Figure 10.3 as well as details corresponding to the related dialog box (see Chapter 5). By writing detailed documentation to accompany the generic code, any additional time required to undertake any modifications to the code will be minimized. In contrast, it would not be efficient to store the simplest of spreadsheet code in a library since the time spent customizing this code to serve any future application may be greater than the time spent on an actual rewrite and test.

PROBLEMS CREATING TEMPLATES AND GENERIC CODE

After determining the basic features that should be incorporated into a generic modelling template, the modeller can adapt the template to a number of modelling applications. Additionally, certain (usually complex) spreadsheet code can be added to the template, and be saved, either in the form of a generic template specific to one modelling application or within a library of reusable code.

However, there may be a number of applications where the development and subsequent use of a modelling template may prove problematic:

- Where the template has been developed from a formal model. This may result in the template housing sections of irrelevant code and references to particular named cells or ranges.
- The template produced may be too restrictive for certain modelling applications, and, in turn, may dictate or simplify the contents of the model.
- The content and style of the generic template may not be agreeable to the end user.

Similarly, the usefulness of code stored in a library for later use may be questionable:

- When the code contains insufficient documentation, especially with regard to variable cell references.
- When the code is too specific to a previous application. If the code is customized, the conversion time may prove prohibitively large.

However, if time is invested, the problems described above can be overcome. Time is especially important with regard to the storing and maintaining of specific sections of spreadsheet code. In developing templates to support specific modelling applications, the problems described may be minimized by developing a suite of modelling skeletons rather than a single template.

TEMPLATE DOCUMENTATION

The importance of documentation should be evident to those modellers wishing to develop either a single skeleton structure or a 'suite' of modelling templates. The format of this documentation should be similar to that used in supporting the development of actual spreadsheet models. Specifically, this documentation should include:

- Internal (or spreadsheet) documentation
- External (or technical) documentation
- A (skeleton) user-guide

Additionally, these self-contained areas should be underpinned by a detailed spreadsheet map, as described in Chapter 7. In short, this template documentation will be a small-scale version of the documentation written to support a formal spreadsheet model. The skeleton documentation should be written in a consistent in-house style and in a way analogous to the production of documentation for an actual model. Moreover, the template documentation can be used as a 'skeleton' when developing actual documentation for future models.

CONCLUSIONS

This chapter has described the development of a generic modelling template and libraries of reusable code. By developing a model skeleton and generic code, it has shown how modeller efficiency may be increased.

However, a single template may be insufficient to support most modelling applications encountered by an individual modeller. Additionally, any template selected should be responsive to the needs of a particular application and *not* vice versa. To adapt to more complex problems, it may be useful to locate the 'model' block in the template as the bottom right-hand block in the skeleton structure. This will permit any modifications to these blocks without major disruption of the rest of the model.

In developing a library of code, the modeller should invest an appropriate amount of time in preparing additional documentation to support the code, specifically identifying any variable cell references or named ranges. Additionally, the modeller must decide which code should be saved and when it would be more efficient to rewrite.

The other areas considered in this chapter are the development of (in-house) customized templates to support specific modelling applications and the availability of commercial spreadsheet models. The advantages and disadvantages of these applications have been addressed.

REVIEW QUESTIONS

1. Describe the advantages and disadvantages of developing a 'suite' of generic modelling templates.
2. Describe the advantages and disadvantages of developing a library of reusable spreadsheet code.
3. List the types of spreadsheet code which should be present in the modelling template.
4. Provide examples of code which should not be incorporated in a modelling template.
5. In 'customizing' a template to a particular modelling application, what criteria must be met by the resultant template?
6. What factors must be considered before purchasing a commercial template to perform a particular modelling application?
7. Assuming the template has adopted a block structure, what are the advantages of locating the model block in the bottom right-hand corner of the skeleton structure?
8. Using a spreadsheet of your choice, construct a modelling template which will be suitable for developing a formal business model. This template should consist of a user-friendly block structure.
9. Add to the modelling template any spreadsheet code which you consider will be common to most future modelling applications.
10. Once this template has been developed, produce the necessary documentation. Save this work and use both the template and documentation when you build any formal model in the future.

GLOSSARY OF TERMS

SPREADSHEET TERMINOLOGY

Auto_Open macro

The Auto_Open macro is the Excel macro which is executed automatically on retrieval of the spreadsheet model. More than one Auto_Open macro can exist in Excel as long as its name starts with Auto_Open. Additionally, another macro, the Auto_Close macro, exists in Excel, and is activated only when the spreadsheet model is closed.

Border suppression

This process involves removing the column and row borders of the spreadsheet, thus enhancing the appearance of the formal model.

Built-in function

A special facility offered by the spreadsheet which performs a specific function. In Excel, a built-in function is entered onto the spreadsheet by first typing = followed by the function word. For example, **AVERAGE( )** is used to calculate the average value for a block of numbers.

Commercial models

These are spreadsheet models written by software companies. The templates are written for a particular spreadsheet and designed for a specific modelling application.

Data security

Security refers to the safety and accessibility of data stored within a spreadsheet model.

Data tables

A data table is a built-in spreadsheet facility which provides a record of the consequence of changing the values of one or two variables within a model. This record can help the model user identify the optimal solution to a modelling situation and also demonstrate how variable the model solution is to changes in the values of the selected parameters.

Dialog box

Dialog boxes are used in Excel to build interfaces between model users and the spreadsheet model. The dialog box can include a list of boxes in which values for input variables can be entered and activated using the relevant macro command.

Goalseek

The goalseek facility permits a model user to determine what value of input for a particular model yields either the known or desired output.

Key combinations

These are combinations of keys which can be utilized to facilitate model navigation.

Lookup tables

A lookup table is a table of data stored in the spreadsheet model. The process of searching this table for relevant information is usually described as 'lookup'. In practice, this type of table will contain data whose values do not change regularly.

Macro

A macro is a set of (related) spreadsheet commands which can be activated automatically by a single keystroke.

Macro buttons

Macro buttons provide a quick and easy way of activating a macro. The model user simply points to the button, clicks on it and the assigned macro is automatically activated.

Macro words

Macro words provide the modeller with a flexible programming facility, permitting the automation of command sequences and keystrokes, facilitating the automation of business functions and providing a method of constructing user–computer interfaces. Examples of macro words considered in this book include **SAVE( ),ARGUMENT( ),DIALOG.BOX( ).**

Memory allocation

This is the method of allocating memory to a spreadsheet model by the spreadsheet. There are three main types of memory allocation:

Sparse matrix Each live cell in the model is allocated memory if this type of allocation is used.

Semi-sparse matrix   If a spreadsheet uses this method, small rectangular blocks of cells are allocated memory, whereas any columns which are completely empty are not allocated any memory.

Dense matrix   For a spreadsheet utilizing dense matrix memory allocation, the top left and bottom right live cells of the model are identified and the rectangle of cells so defined are allocated memory.

In practice, memory allocation is a problem most often encountered by modellers using older spreadsheets.

Navigational macros

This type of macro facilitates the efficient movement of the model user from block to block within the structured model.

Operational macros

Operational macros are those sections of spreadsheet code which deal with automating the routines of data input, manipulation and output.

Scenario Manager

This is an Excel facility which permits a modeller to store and analyse information pertaining to a range of different modelling scenarios.

Spreadsheet

A spreadsheet is a software program which consists of rows and columns which combine to form a grid of cells. Each cell on the spreadsheet grid can contain text, numbers or formulae. By combining text, numbers and formulae in an appropriate way, the software can be used to model a wide range of business problems.

Spreadsheet map

This map is a diagrammatical representation of a proposed spreadsheet model and should be used as a blueprint for any subsequent spreadsheet development.

Workbook

A set of related Excel spreadsheets usually consisting of a front cover, model sheet and macro sheets.

MODELLING TERMINOLOGY

Analog model

This model represents the features of the problem under consideration by different features of the model.

Block structure

A method of model design where the discrete sections of the model are allocated separate, self-contained blocks. In practice, these blocks should have dimensions of whole numbers of screens.

Conceptual model

A conceptual model is used primarily to transform a (business) problem into a mathematical model. In reality, a conceptual model is a diagrammatical display of the problem under consideration, which makes the distinction between input, process and output variables.

Descriptive model

A descriptive model is used to describe either the existing or desired situation providing the model user with an opportunity to explore a number of different scenarios. In permitting this, they allow an end user to ask 'what if' questions about the modelling situation.

End-user experimentation

This is the process where the end user can utilize the model to explore a number of possible scenarios with respect to the problem situation. Many modellers recognize that the greatest asset of the spreadsheet is its 'user-friendliness' and its ability to facilitate end-user experimentation.

External (technical) documentation

The spreadsheet model's external documentation is written for those who will monitor the performance of and, where necessary, update the model. As a consequence, the external documentation is a technical reference, and therefore must be written in spreadsheet terminology.

Formulae

The formulae are the mathematical expressions which are used to represent the relationships that exist between the variables in the (spreadsheet) model.

Help block

The on-screen help facilities play an important role in supporting the use of a structured model. In practice, such facilities may incorporate instructions on menu use and model navigation.

Iconic model

This model is a physical and (usually) scaled representation of a problem.

Implementation

Implementation is the acceptance of the model into the decision-making process within an organization. The degree of success achieved in implementing a particular model will be influenced mainly by the confidence shown in both its user-friendliness and its output by the end user.

Influence diagrams

An influence diagram is a diagrammatical display of the decisions, variables and relationships between variables that relate to a modelling problem. The influence diagram is a particularly useful tool for converting the business problem into a formal model. In this diagram distinction is made between input, process and output and those relationships which are definite and indefinite.

Input block

This block contains those variables whose values are likely to alter with each application of the model. In contrast, other parameters used in the model whose values are non-variable can be hard-coded.

Internal (spreadsheet) documentation

The internal documentation of a spreadsheet model takes the form of comments written on the spreadsheet adjacent to the relevant (spreadsheet) code. The role of these comments is to clarify the meaning of each individual section of code whose aims may be unclear to the end user.

Introduction block

The introductory screen provides the model user with an overview of the model's role and is arguably the most important area of the program from the point of view of an end user with limited spreadsheet experience.

Libraries of reusable code

A library of reusable code refers to code stored either as paper or as a text file on computer which may be used in future modelling applications. This type of code will usually consist of complex routines. The advantage of saving such routines is that time is saved re-writing the code and, as a result, modeller efficiency can be enhanced.

Macro sheet

This sheet, which is separate from the spreadsheet housing the spreadsheet model, contains all of the macro code which is activated by a user of the spreadsheet model.

Macro documentation

This process involves naming and describing the macro code on the (macro) sheet in order to facilitate both modeller and end-user understanding. A useful method of macro documentation involves utilizing a two-column format, where the first column contains the macro code and the second the detailed line-by-line documentation.

Mathematical model

A mathematical model uses mathematical formulae to describe the relationships that exist between the different variables in a business problem.

Model

A model is a simplified illustration of a real situation.

Model block

The model block represents the internal processes of the program. That is, this block contains the mathematical relationships which represent the business problem and have been identified from the conceptual model.

Model robustness

Robustness refers to how well a model can withstand improper use by an end user with limited spreadsheet experience, e.g. how well it can respond to an end user accidentally erasing or writing over some of the spreadsheet code.

Model template

This is a model skeleton based on a block structure which contains generic spreadsheet code such as navigational macros and screen titles, which are common to most or all modelling applications.

Model test data

This is the set of data which is used to support the validation and verification process. In general, there are three categories of data which should be developed:

- Inappropriate or unexpected data for each input variable
- Simple data to facilitate the verification of each relationship represented in the spreadsheet model
- Data sets which can normally be associated with the process under consideration.

Model user-guide

This provides instructions for an end user regarding how to use the spreadsheet model. Because the model may be aimed at an end user with limited spreadsheet experience, the guide should not use spreadsheet terminology, but non-technical English.

On-screen mapping details

This is another help facility which may be incorporated into a formal model. This block provides a map of the spreadsheet model, which may be a diagrammatical representation of the model, a set of cell references, or a combination of diagram and cell references.

Optimization

Optimization is the process whereby a model user can identify and utilize the 'best' possible solution to a business problem.

Prescriptive model

A prescriptive model is deterministic in nature and often includes the use of algorithms. The aim of a prescriptive model is to provide the model user with a 'best' answer to the problem under consideration.

Problem conceptualization

This involves the modeller determining what decision(s) need to be made, the variables which have to be considered, the behaviour of these variables and their interrelationships.

Results (Output) block

This block contains the model's output and, as a result, will be of most interest to the model user. This information will be utilized by the model user to solve the problem under consideration.

Sensitivity analysis

Sensitivity analysis involves determining the extent that a model's output may vary in response to changes in value of one or more of the model's parameters.

Top-down method

This is a method which can be used to write large or complex programs. The method involves the programmer starting with a broad plan of the problem, which is written in English rather than program code. Detail is then incorporated into this general plan until coding becomes possible.

Validation

Model validation is an investigation into how effectively the model can represent the real process. In other words, a measure of a model's validity is its ability to duplicate known results.

Verification

Verification is the process in which the logic and consistency of the (spreadsheet) code is considered.

'What if' analysis

In measuring the sensitivity of a model's output, the end user undertakes 'what if' analysis. 'What if' analysis is the process whereby a number of possible business scenarios can be explored by utilizing the model.

MATHEMATICAL AND STATISTICAL TERMINOLOGY

Data analysis

The term given to the process of examining a data set by using appropriate statistical and graphical techniques.

Frequency distribution

A graph or table which displays the number of times a particular variable occurs within a set of intervals.

Net present value (NPV)

A method of investment appraisal which enables a future set of cashflows to be expressed in terms of present money value.

Scatter diagram

An XY graph where the points are not connected by a line. A modeller can determine from the shape of the points on a scatter diagram what type of relationship exists, if any, between two variables.

Simple regression model

A simple regression model is used to measure and quantify a relationship between a variable of interest known as a dependent variable and a measurable or independent variable. The simple regression model is based on the equation of 'best' straight line between the points on a scatter diagram.

Summary statistics

Summary or descriptive statistics are those measures which give an indication about the typical values of each variable in the data set (e.g. mean) and an indication of spread for each variable in the data set (e.g. standard deviation). In Excel, there are a number of built-in statistical commands (as well as a comprehensive Analysis Toolkit) which can be used to provide well-established summary statistics.

INDEX